SELLING WITH MOMENTUM

A Success Mentality for New Home Sales

By Richard Tiller

D1194729

Printed in the U.S.A. by Tiller Marketing Services
P.O. Box 531
Herndon, VA. 20172-0531

Contents

Introduction

In 1991 I wrote a book entitled *Success in New Home Sales,* based upon my experiences as a new home salesperson, sales and marketing manager, and industry participant from 1972 to 1991. That same year I began my current profession as a one-on-one consultant to salespeople. Each day I work with one or more salespeople at the communities where they sell. We discuss ways to handle the challenges they believe they must overcome in order to achieve the next level of success in their own personal careers. Since 1991 I have completed more than four thousand site visits with individual salespeople. Almost every day I learn something new as our brainstorming produces a fresh idea, technique, attitude or insight – or perhaps a subtly different application of an old one. From this work comes a second book about what it takes to be successful in new home sales.

The fundamentals of successful selling have not changed profoundly in the past twelve years, because people's fundamental needs, motivations and characteristics have not changed profoundly. We are more technologically sophisticated than we were a decade ago, but that can be said about every decade for the past century. The basic nature of our species does not change quickly. This book is therefore not an attempt to reinvent the selling wheel. As in *Success in New Home Sales,* I will emphasize the roles of momentum, rapport, need fulfillment, concept selling, and the selling process as a whole.

In *Success in New Home Sales* I tried to balance the importance of mentality and skills in successful selling. In fact, the subtitle of that book was *Developing the Right Mentality and Techniques.* Here I will take a similar approach, but with a little more emphasis on a **success mentality.** I will explore how the most successful salespeople think, and how they transform their thoughts into skills. While this book gives many examples of how salespeople sell though their words, it also explores the thought processes behind these words. If we know how to think, we can figure out how to act and what to say. This book does not unveil a secret formula for success or a magic bullet. It explores the thoughts and skills that separate top new home salespeople from the rest, and how they maximize more of their opportunities.

Some of the ideas in this book find their origins in *Success in New Home Sales.* Other information is taken from *New Home Sales Insights,* a monthly newsletter I published throughout the 1990's. And much of it is new.

Here are some of the areas in which this book is intended to provide help:

1. Building productive relationships with customers.

2. Creating the best and most enriching experience possible for every prospect with whom you work.

3. Advancing the sale from one stage to the next, and maximizing the opportunities in each stage.

4. Maintaining a position of strength under any conditions.

5. Handling objections and other sales challenges.

6. Closing with skill and confidence.

7. Following up comfortably and productively.

8. Managing customers before and after the contract.

9. Surviving the up-and-down nature of the sales profession.

10. Developing your own mentality for success.

The opportunity to work one-on-one with so many different salespeople over the years has been an inspiring, uplifting, and immensely enriching experience for me. I hope that through this book I will be able to share with you the knowledge, joy and enrichment these salespeople have given to me.

A Success Mentality

If you study the careers of those new home salespeople who have achieved the highest level of success over the longest period of time, you will find that the characteristics upon which they built their success fall under four basic categories:

1.   Success Mentality
2.   Skills
3.   Energy
4.   Temperament

Throughout this book we will be looking at what each of these categories means in a successful new home sales career. In this chapter we will explore the first category above: What does it mean to have "success mentality?" What kind of thought process provides the strong foundation upon which a successful career can be built? Here are several ways that the winners in new home sales think about selling in order to gain their competitive edge.

SELLING SHOULD FEEL EASY

A success mentality begins with the idea that selling a home to a customer is a completely natural interaction. The relationship between a salesperson and a customer is a normal human relationship. In our business, unlike some other forms of selling, nothing ever needs to be contrived. The principles that make a relationship succeed between a new home salesperson and a customer are the same principles that make other kinds of relationships succeed.

A success mentality also includes the belief that selling new homes is as easy as it is natural. The more clearheaded you are in your approach to selling, the more successful you will be. In selling, simplicity is your friend, complexity your enemy. You must never create complexity. When you are faced with it, your goal is to simplify it. The reason simplicity is so important in new home sales is that you are helping customers make decisions. The more complicated a decision becomes, the more difficult it is to make. Making decisions with confidence requires uncluttered thinking. You must help customers simplify their thoughts and maintain their focus in order to help them make decisions with conviction. For many customers buying a home is very complicated. It is not the kind of decision they make very often, and they are not experts at the building or buying process (even though some may think they are). As a salesperson, your mission is to take that which is complex and make it simple.

ESTABLISH AND MAINTAIN MOMENTUM

A success mentality focuses on momentum throughout the sale. Momentum is a key force in new home sales. It is the force that propels the selling process. Selling is not merely a random occurrence. It is a planned process – *a series of objectives that lead to a series of decisions.*

A number of years ago I worked with a salesperson who achieved success very quickly in her career, and then sustained that success as her career progressed. I asked her what she thought made her so successful. Her answer beautifully summarized the energy of the selling process. She said, "There are two things about me that have made me successful. The first is that whatever stage of the sale I'm in, I always know what I'm going to do next. The second is that I have a compulsive need to resolve things." Her way of approaching a sale demonstrated a mindset for momentum.

Throughout the selling process, your goal is to keep the sale moving from one stage to the next, resolving issues and decisions along the way. Each time you meet a customer, you want to generate momentum as quickly as possible, and then keep that momentum going as long as possible. Whatever stage of the sale you are in, your goal is always to get to the next stage. To achieve this goal you need a plan for how to build a bridge from one stage to the next.

There are seven primary objectives in the selling process:

1. Establish rapport with your customer.

2. Convey your selling message.

3. Identify your customer's needs.

4. Show how your homes fulfill those needs.

5. Lead the customer to choose a favorite home.

6. Lead the customer to choose a favorite home site.

7. Ask for the sale.

As you accomplish each objective you are setting the stage for the next – creating a situation in which the customer wants to keep going. We often wonder, "How can I maintain control of the sale?" *You will have control of the sale as long as the customer wants to go farther.* So the way to stay in control of the selling environment is to get the customer to want to keep going.

It is important that, as a salesperson, you are never the one who stops the sale. Consciously you know you always want to keep the sale moving, so you assume that whenever a sale stops, it must be the customer who stops it. But in fact, you may be stopping the sale more often than you realize. Perhaps you feel you aren't making the progress you want, so you shut it down. Sometimes it is because the customer is not responding with the enthusiasm you hope for. However, they may not really want to stop the sale. Perhaps they simply have not yet developed a "momentum mentality" of their own. In this case their responses appear passive, yet they are willing to follow if you are willing to lead. The most successful salespeople always try to maintain a position of leadership in their relationship with their customers.

Regardless of a customer's demeanor or emotions, assume they want to go farther until they tell you they do not. If they are still in your presence, take that as a "yes." *Only the customer should stop the sale, never the salesperson.* This is one of the simplest principles in new home sales, yet it is also one of the most important. Try to keep every sale moving until the customer tells you it is impossible for them to go any farther.

SELL TO A STRANGER AS YOU WOULD SELL TO A FRIEND

One of the easiest ways to develop a momentum mentality is to ask, "How would I sell a home to my best friend?" If you look at selling from this perspective, everything else about the process falls into place much more easily. Let's play this idea out and see where it goes.

Your best friend is looking for a new home. Knowing that you sell homes, she expresses a desire to see your community. You feel that your homes might be exactly what she needs, so you invite her to see them. Once she arrives at your sales office, how would you handle the situation?

First, you would want to make the experience comfortable for her. You don't want her to buy a home that is not right for her. But you are proud of your homes, and you don't know of any reason why she shouldn't buy one. While no home is "perfect" for any buyer, you truly believe that your friend will not find a better home for her money anywhere else. You want to help your friend understand and appreciate your homes, community and builder. To assure that she does appreciate everything you offer, you create a plan for her visit, and you want to accomplish as much of your plan as possible before she leaves.

You want to understand her needs. You would ask the questions necessary to learn those needs.

You want her to know why you believe one of your homes would be good for her. You would explain why other people have chosen your homes, and why you like them. In establishing credibility for your homes and your builder, your enthusiasm is as important as your knowledge.

You want to accompany her through your homes. If she goes alone, she will not get the most out of the experience, because she will not know how. You also want to know how she reacts and what she thinks as she goes through. As you accompany your friend, you can explain what makes your homes and builder different, and go into more vivid detail about the design, quality and features that cause people to choose your homes. You can also get continuous feedback, answering questions and addressing concerns as you go. Naturally you do not want to pressure your friend to buy your home if it is not right for her, or if she is truly not ready to make a decision. However, you assume she could make a decision if she finds a home she likes, even though she may need your help to make that decision. After all, she is the one who came to you with a desire to improve her life. Therefore, without any pressure, you want to keep her on track and focused.

If your friend finds a home she likes, your next step is to help her resolve her decision. The sooner she can reach a decision, the sooner her life will improve. For that reason, you would try to close her. Not because you are a good closer, but because your friend would expect it. Your friend will tell you if she's not ready, or if she thinks it's not the right decision. Your job is simply to keep things moving. If you don't, she will wonder what is wrong.

That is the way you would sell a home to a friend – easy and natural. Selling to a stranger works the same way. This is the selling process in a nutshell. It does not need to be overly orchestrated or contrived. However, it does require some planning. As with the salesperson we discussed earlier, you establish momentum in the selling process by:

1. Being prepared – knowing how you will get your customer

to the next stage – and,

2. Resolving issues and decisions along the way.

CREATE AN ENRICHING EXPERIENCE

There has been much debate over the question of how much difference a salesperson can really make in the success of a community. The truth is that a salesperson can make a huge difference in many ways: increasing the sales volume, increasing the profit per unit, contributing to the efficiency of the overall field operation, providing sales and marketing feedback to management, helping achieve a higher level of customer satisfaction, and enhancing the overall image of the company. In the actual face-to-face selling process with customers, one of the most important ways that outstanding salespeople win sales from average ones is by creating a more enriching experience for the prospective buyers who visit their homes.

Top salespeople energize the atmosphere around them, and thereby energize their customers as well. Energy is part of a mentality for success. One salesperson with whom I worked put it this way: "I know I'm not going to sell a home to everyone who walks in the door, so I've set a different goal for myself. I want every person I work with, whether they wind up buying a home from me or not, to walk away saying, 'That was the best salesperson I ever met.'" This fellow conveyed his special energy to his customers, and energized many of them as a result. He is a terrific example of a salesperson who earnestly seeks to create a more enriching experience for his customers than his competition can create.

Here are several ways you can create a more enriching experience.

1. Show your personal interest in each customer.

Customers need to feel valued, not only as customers but also as people. They need to feel a sense of respect and dignity in your presence. Mutual respect and dignity are as important in a selling relationship as in any other human relationship. Customers want to know that their interaction with you is meaningful to you as well as to them.

If customers are willing to talk to you, make them feel good about it. Respond with interest to what they say. Let them talk as much as possible about themselves, their situation, their needs, and what has inspired them to begin looking for a new home. Some customers are less willing to talk than others. Whenever customers do begin to talk, make them feel glad they did. We learn from the world of psychology, "If you want to create a pattern of behavior, reward the behavior when it occurs at random."

Some customers may not want to talk at first, but are still willing to listen. In that case, go ahead with an overview of what you are selling and why people are buying it, and then see if they are more willing to open up as their comfort level increases. If they insist on going through the models alone, then use time as your friend by giving them some space for awhile. You can try again later to get things going, after they have had a chance to look around. In any event, use every opportunity possible to show your interest in them, and in fulfilling their needs.

2. Be a counselor instead of a salesperson.

Customers need counselors more than they need salespeople. You don't need to sell them a home in the first five minutes. This time is better spent building trust and creating a non-threatening environment. Before you try to actively start selling, let them know that you are an expert who cares about fulfilling their needs. As mentioned above, if they do not want to give you information about themselves at first, you can still begin to set a constructive tone by saying, "Before you see our homes, let me give you a quick overview of what we're doing here."

3. Show your own enthusiasm.

Showing enthusiasm does not require acrobatics. It simply means showing your customers that you are happy selling your homes, being in your community and working for your builder. The more your customers see that you are happy with your job, and the more they see that you believe in it, the more confident and comfortable they will be with you and with what you have to say. Enthusiasm really is contagious, but so is the lack of it.

4. Convey a selling message.

A selling message does not have to be mundane, scripted or eternally repetitious, but it must be consistent. Everyone who could possibly be a candidate for one of your homes needs to hear what you think makes your homes special, and why people choose them over all of the other available alternatives. A consistent selling message is a critical element in providing a more enriching experience. We will discuss this idea in detail in our next chapter.

5. Create anticipation for what lies ahead.

We said earlier that you have control of the selling environment as long as the customer wants to go farther. Maintaining your selling momentum with a customer involves creating a positive sense of anticipation in the buyer's mind for what lies ahead, so that they will want to keep going. Look for opportunities in each stage of the sale for whetting the customer's appetite to learn more about your company, your community, your homes and your home sites.

6. Use your visits to models and home sites to build relationships and fulfill needs.

When you leave the environment of the sales office and move away to either the models or the site, the potential for enrichment increases. The models and site provide many opportunities beyond merely the demonstration of features and benefits. You have the opportunity to build your relationship with your customers. You can learn more about them and their needs while they learn more about you, your company and your homes.

7. Stay focused on decisions.

The buying process is a series of decisions – small ones leading to larger ones. A customer's most important buying signal is the ability and willingness to make decisions. Your focus is helping customers make these decisions, one at a time. Ask feedback questions along the way, and use this feedback constructively. Help your customers resolve one issue at a time. Resolving issues and making decisions lead to closing. Even closing is a part of the enrichment process. After all, making the right decision is ultimately the most enriching part of the buying experience.

8. Let them know you want them as a customer.

This is another one of those obvious things we sometimes forget. Even if a customer is not prepared to make a decision that day, you can still say, "I've really enjoyed getting to spend some time with you, and I hope we get to have you as a customer." If your visitors hear those words from you and not from your competitors, then you have differentiated yourself from everyone else in one more way.

9. Establish a way to maintain contact.

When you conclude your interaction, you can also add, "If it's okay with you, I'd like to give you a call to follow up." Now you no longer need to worry about contriving a reason to make a follow up call. The customer expects it as part of your diligent effort to provide a more complete service.

10. Maintain a positive attitude in all situations.

In addition to showing your enthusiasm, a positive attitude can make a difference in other ways as well. For some people, buying a new home can mean traveling a bumpy road, at least for a while. Many customers experience anxiety at some point during the buying process or the construction process. If they see you with a consistently positive attitude, it can reassure them of a happy ending that will be worth the effort. Your positive attitude is sometimes a customer's primary source of hope and stability. After all, you have traveled this road many more times than they have, and have seen many situations work out better than customers thought they would.

MAINTAIN AN ABUNDANCE MENTALITY

Confidence is an essential part of a success mentality in any endeavor. In selling, one form of confidence is an **abundance mentality** – a feeling of assurance that there is plenty of business to go around, regardless of market conditions. It is the feeling that if you do a good job, the sales will come.

Part of an abundance mentality is realizing that sometimes it is okay to lose a sale. In fact, the willingness to lose a sale may sometimes be your greatest position of strength, just as the fear that you can never afford to lose a sale can create a position of weakness. Selling scared is treacherous. Customers can feel it.

Statistically, the majority of people who visit your community will never buy a home from you. That's okay, because you can't build homes fast enough or buy enough lots to provide a home for everyone who walks in your door anyway. Your homes were never designed or priced to be for everyone. If someone doesn't want your home, it's not the end of the world. It happens to every salesperson every day. It doesn't mean your homes are bad or overpriced or uncompetitive. You will have plenty of opportunities to sell every home you build. It is important not to get discouraged.

Admittedly, it can be frustrating to spend a lot of time and effort on a prospect that doesn't buy, especially when you feel as though you got so close. It's like getting a triple in baseball and then not scoring a run. Sometimes a triple simply does not convert into a run scored. But a triple is still a good hit, and, in the long run, the more triples you hit the more runs you will score.

When customers see that you are not afraid to lose a sale, they frequently become impressed and encouraged by your confidence. Your own confidence may transfer to them and increase their comfort level about buying your home. It is not arrogance or carelessness, just a gentle confidence in yourself, your homes and your company, and a belief that if you give every customer your best effort, all of your homes will be sold by the time your company needs them to be. When customers see that you are comfortable and relaxed with your attitude toward yourself and what you are selling, it will become easier for you to generate the kind of selling momentum you are seeking in your relationship with them.

PREPARE YOUR GAME PLAN

I have talked about the salesperson who attributed her success to "always knowing what to do next" and "having a compulsive desire to resolve things." Here I would like to discuss her first comment a little more. In her spare time she did a lot of planning for how she would take a role of leadership in her relationships with her customers and lead them through the selling process one step at a time. Her goal was always to resolve each stage with feedback and decisions, and create a positive sense of anticipation for the next one. She tried to envision as many scenarios as possible, and plan what she would say and do in advance, so that it would feel easy and natural when the time arrived. Developing a leadership role in your relationships with customers requires planning and preparation. A proactive approach to leading customers through the selling process is part of a mentality for success.

Preparation occurs at two levels. First there is preparation for your overall success. This includes:

- Knowing your product – features (standard and optional), benefits and construction techniques.

- Knowing your competition – how their product compares with yours, your advantages over them, their advantages over you, and how you plan to counter their advantages if you have to.

- Understanding your company's paperwork – the paper itself and the process for implementing it.

- Understanding the kinds of financing that are available, and the qualification standards that lenders use.

- Understanding your company's policies, and its expectations of salespeople in terms of performance, responsibilities and standards.

The second kind of preparation would be your plan for handling the customers who walk in your door – how you will get them from one stage of the sale to the next until their buying decision is resolved, one way or the other.

Building Relationships With Customers

When a customer visits your community for the first time, your initial goal is to provide the most enjoyable and enriching experience possible. You want to make your customers feel good about you, and you want to help them feel good about themselves. In addition, you use the greeting stage of the sale to:

- Begin building a relationship with customers.
- Learn their needs, priorities, motivations and level of urgency.
- Determine their qualifications.
- Give an overview of what you are selling, including a selling message.

The greeting is the springboard of the sale. In this chapter we will see how each of the elements of a success mentality comes into play at the beginning of the sale: simplicity, momentum, selling to a stranger like a friend, creating an enriching experience, conveying an abundance mentality, and preparing a strategy for the first few minutes that is designed to get the selling process on to a productive track.

BREAKING THE ICE

The greeting should feel natural, not contrived. A natural, social greeting sets up the selling process in an easier, more comfortable way. If you were greeting someone in a social setting, such as a party, you might introduce yourself, smile warmly, shake hands, express your pleasure in meeting the person, and perhaps ask a non-threatening question to start a conversation. You can greet a customer in much the same way.

In selling, you can use social questions to lead into your "qualifying" questions. Your sequence of questions could evolve as follows, depending upon the customer's responses.

"Hi, I'm _____."...[Wait for them to respond with their name.]...*"It's a pleasure to meet you. Thanks for coming out. Do you folks live nearby?"*...*"Are you thinking of making a move?"*...*"What has gotten you thinking about moving?"*...*"Do you have a particular time frame in mind (price range, kind of home, etc.)?"*...*"Are you familiar with this area (with this community, with our company, etc.)?"*...*"Let me give you an overview of what we're doing here..."*

Here you are moving into the area of learning the customer's primary motivations and needs, so that as the sale progresses, you can go about the business of fulfilling their needs. You also want to try to find out if they are a "ready, willing and able" buyer. Are they in a position to buy one of your homes – financially, circumstantially and emotionally – if they find one they like?

Instead of a rapid-fire sequence of qualifying questions, work your questions into the conversation throughout the greeting. Ask questions that will lead easily into follow up questions. For example:

- *"Are you familiar with this area?...How do you like it?...Does this location work for you?...Are you considering any other areas?"*
- *"What kind of home do you live in now?...How do you like it?...Are you looking for something different?...In what ways*

do you want your next home to be different than the one you live in now?"

- *"Do you have a particular kind of home in mind that you're looking for?...Is there anything that's a top priority for you?"*

- *"How has your search been going so far?...Have you seen anything that you've especially liked?"*

- *"How are you feeling about the whole idea of moving?"*

Here are some other questions that may become useful if the conversation is going in the appropriate direction:

- *"What sort of things are important to you in a location?"*

- *"Do you work in this area?"* *("Where do you work?")*

- *"What kind of work do you do?"* [Be sure to show interest in their work.]

- *"Is there anything controlling your timetable?...If you found a home you really liked, would that make a difference?"*

- *"Are you planning to sell your current home?...Do you have it on the market yet?"*

- *"Are you just beginning your search, or have you been looking for a while?"*

- [For first-time buyers]: *"Has anyone ever explained to you how it (the process) works when you buy a home?"* [Related to this question would be]: *"Has anyone ever explained to you how the financing works when you buy a home?...Would you like a five-minute crash course?"* [These are questions that help you establish a counselor relationship that is based on trust, service and expertise. This is what many first-time buyers need in order to develop the confidence to begin taking steps toward a buying decision.]

- *"Do you know the size of your current home?...Do you know the size you'd like your next home to be?"* [For these two questions, don't ask about the square footage at first. Let them answer in terms of what "size" means to them – whether they feel size is square footage, number of bedrooms, or some other priority.]

- *"Do you have children?"* [If they do, be sure to show interest in their children. It is a compliment, and can lead into questions about the kind of home that would meet their needs.]
- *"Do you have any special activities or interests that will be a factor in the kind of home (community) you choose?"*

A CUSTOMER'S NEEDS CAN CHANGE, AND SO CAN THEIR PLANS

The sooner you can begin to understand a customer's needs, the more quickly you can go about the business of fulfilling those needs. Sometimes it will become clear that none of your homes will ever be able to fulfill their needs. You know it without a doubt, and you realize there is no point in prolonging a futile effort. On the other hand, sometimes you see the possibility that their needs and priorities are not yet set in stone. In these situations, you want to explore the possibility of helping them reevaluate and redefine their needs.

One way you can do this is by showing how your homes have fulfilled the needs of others. The use of anecdotes and third-party endorsements is tremendously valuable in selling new homes. Telling about the opinions and experiences of others can help bring your unique value to life for your customers, and give them a reality to which they can relate. Anecdotes and third-party endorsements also give credibility to your market position. You can explain why you designed your homes and community the way you did, and why other people have chosen you over your competition.

While it is important to ask questions in order to identify and fulfill needs, there are four reasons for not always accepting your customer's initial needs list too passively:

1. Customers do not always distinguish between needs and fleeting wants.
2. They may not yet be fully educated as to what their needs

should be.

3. Even though their current home is not meeting their needs, no one else can meet them either.

4. Customers' needs frequently change as they go through the buying process.

Some of us have occasionally turned customers away because we believed we could not fulfill their needs, and then watched them buy from a competitor who offered a very similar home. The difference may have been the competitor's willingness to go that extra step to help customers rethink what their needs really should be.

While customers' needs can change as they go through the buying process, so can their plans. Sometimes customers walk in your door with no plan at all. They're "just looking." Other times they do have a plan, but their plan does not seem to fit with what you are selling. As with fulfilling needs, don't lose heart when, at first glance, it looks as though your availability does not fit their plans. *Just as customers' needs often change as they go through the buying process, customers often change their plans when they find a home they want.*

When a customer presents you with a game plan that poses serious obstacles, but you believe it is not hopeless, you can respond to them like this: *"I certainly understand what you're saying. As long as you're here, I can show you what we do have and explain why so many people have bought here."* Then continue on with the business of presenting the concept, features and benefits of your homes. If your mission really is hopeless, they will tell you. As long as they don't tell you it's hopeless, you should be broadening their horizons and giving them additional food for thought.

Top salespeople win many of their sales by going just a little farther with customers upon whom they could have given up. Some sales are predictable based on the original information the customer reveals. However, many other sales wind up being surprises, which result from the customer's willingness to change their plans because they found a home worth changing for.

BUILDING RAPPORT TAKES FLEXIBILITY

When you set out to establish rapport with your customers, you sometimes face the challenge that they are not as interested in establishing rapport as you are. Don't be discouraged. A lot can change during the course of a customer's visit.

While some customers are willing to talk your ears off from the moment they walk in the door, others are not so cooperative. They may want only to see your models and be left alone. Don't think of building rapport as a battle of wills that you have to win. Instead, assume at the outset that when it comes to establishing rapport, you will have three different types of situations for which to plan. To prepare for each of these situations, let's call our strategies Plan A, Plan B and Plan C.

The Plan A situation involves the customer who comes to your community with a sense of purpose and a desire to talk about it. At the greeting stage, Plan A prospects are our favorites. With them you may choose to just go with the flow, as long as the process is going in the general direction you want it to. You can feel free to change your sequence to meet the needs the customer expresses, as long as their sense of purpose seems genuine. If they tell you that the home site is more important to them than the home, and you feel that they would not be able to focus on your homes until they understand the kinds of home sites you are offering, you can go right to the home site stage of the sale. You can come back later to your presentation of your homes, builder and selling message. As long as you keep an eye on the overall progress of the sale, you can allow the customer to lead for a while. However, you may sometimes have to see if they are willing to redefine their needs.

At the opposite end of the spectrum is the Plan C situation. This is where the customer is totally rude and uncooperative. They brush past you, avoid eye contact, won't answer your questions, and are insulting in their demeanor. There is no way you can plan on winning in this situation at the beginning. Let the customer go through the model, and see if there is a chance they might warm up to you later. Use time as your friend and not your enemy. Even though you can't establish rapport at the beginning, you may be more successful after the customer begins to feel a little more at home. You can always just say, *"Make yourself at home,"* up front, and then catch up with them in the model later to see if you can be of any assistance. Then you could ask them, *"Would you like me to tell you a little about our community?"* or, *"Would you like me to give you a quick overview of what we're doing here?"* If they say, "No," it is reasonable to assume they are probably not very good prospects at that point. However, if they say, "Yes," then the door may finally be opening for you to begin building your rapport. Realistically, we have to assume that the Plan C situation will yield a very small percent of your sales, although a few will surprise you with their turnaround.

The situation where your individual approach can make the biggest difference is the Plan B situation. This is where top salespeople most often win sales away from average ones. In many markets, the Plan B buyers are actually the ones we see most often. These buyers are not rude, but also do not seem focused. They just seem mildly disoriented, and this is quite understandable. They walk in saying something like, "We're just looking. Do you have a brochure?" The fact that they are "just looking" is not a bad thing. It may simply mean they don't know what else to say. You don't have to think of them as a buyer just yet. For the moment, you can start out by just thinking of them as people.

When we meet a stranger at a social function, we often start out by asking them where they're from. We are socially trained that this is a natural icebreaker, because most people feel comfortable talking about where they're from. It is a socially acceptable way of getting a new acquaintance to open up. The same can be true in sales. You can start out by simply asking your "guest" where they're from. Then you can ask how they like it there. From there you can move very naturally to the question, *"Are you thinking of making a move?"* Once they answer that question it becomes very easy to ask, *"What is it that's gotten you thinking about moving?"* You are now comfortably into your qualifying questions that can, in turn, lead to further questions about price range, time frame and product preferences. Questions about occupation and family are also very natural icebreakers that you can use in a business setting as well. You can use social questions to lead into your qualifying questions.

But what about the Plan B buyers who are not rude, but also not very forthcoming? They aren't pushing you away, but their answers to your questions are brief, vague and unhelpful. Remember that some people who do not communicate with much enthusiasm or clarity in the beginning are nevertheless willing to listen to what you have to say. If your questions are not getting you anywhere, you can switch gears and say to the customer, *"Let me tell you a little about what we're doing here."* You can move right into your overview and selling message, and see how they respond. Your selling message may be a critical piece of the puzzle for this buyer. Some people just want you to tell them about your homes while they listen. That is what they came in for, and there is nothing weird about that. Once they decide your homes may be worth considering, and once they begin to get a comfortable feeling about you, they may become more willing to open up a little. Again, use time as your friend. Let them see you as professional, knowledgeable and helpful, while they become more comfortable with their surroundings.

When customers do begin to open up, make them glad they did. Respond with appreciation and interest to everything they say. This is the best way to get them to open up more. Responding to customers can be a more effective tool for building rapport than trying to pry interaction out of them with aggressive interrogation. Responding shows that you are listening to them, and that you are interested in them. *If you want to make customers feel good about you, be the one who makes them feel good about themselves.*

THE SELLING MESSAGE IS AS IMPORTANT AS EVER

We have talked about providing a more enriching experience than your competition. Part of this experience is an enriching selling message. Rigid "canned presentations" can cause you to miss opportunities to establish personal rapport with your customers, and also to identify and fulfill their specific needs. However, parts of your presentation need to remain consistent in order for your level of impact to remain consistent. One of these elements is your basic selling message. Left to our own devices, some of us tend to neglect those parts of our presentation that we get tired of. We repeat a point again and again, and it begins to sound mundane to us. But we have to remember that the customer is hearing it for the first time. An outstanding salesperson once said to me, "I don't want a canned presentation, but I do want a canned minute. I want a strong impact statement that will be meaningful to everyone – a message so strong that it will always make the customer want to hear more."

Let's consider three basic questions concerning a consistent selling message.

1. Why is a selling message so important?

2. What exactly is a selling message?

3. Where does a selling message come from?

The reason a selling message is so important is that it helps shape your customer's thought process about what you are selling. It carves out your own particular space in the customer's mind. It causes them to think differently about you than they think about everyone else. Your selling message tells them why they should consider your home.

CONCEPT SELLING

Your selling message is your basic mission statement. It is the overall *concept* of what you are selling. The reason it is important to articulate your concept is that the human brain likes thinking about concepts more than it likes thinking about features and benefits. People think more easily on a conceptual level. While features and benefits are an important part of selling, they have more impact if the customer can think of them within the context of a larger concept.

The idea of concept selling is an easy one. In fact, once you think about it, concept selling becomes the easiest way to explain what makes your homes special, different and better. You always face the challenge of showing your customers why they should choose your homes over all of the other alternatives that are available to them in the marketplace. When your company first conceptualized your community, they had to wrestle with this same question in order to establish a competitive market position that could win the desired number of sales.

Start out by sitting down with the managers who were involved at the beginning of the project and ask them what they believe your market position is. That is where your selling message – or concept – originates. It comes from your *market position.* To develop a selling message, begin by trying to put your market position into a sentence or two – a short statement that explains why you feel a customer will choose you over all the other alternatives in the marketplace.

In new home sales, your concept is *a concise statement of your product's unique significance – why your product is important in the marketplace.* In marketing terms, your concept is your *positioning statement.* In selling terms, it is an *impact statement.* It helps the customer to focus quickly on *why your homes are special and why they have been selling* (or, at the beginning of a community, *why you believe they will sell*). It tells your customers *why your homes are best.* This kind of statement can give you a competitive advantage, because while many salespeople may make a statement of why their homes are good, most do not make a statement of why their homes are best.

Your selling message is also a ***value statement***. Every product defines value in a slightly different way, because each was designed and priced with a slightly different set of priorities. How does your product define value?

Why was your product designed the way it was in the first place? Why does it exist? What needs were your homes designed to fulfill? In what ways are your homes better than the competition? What puts them in a category apart from everyone else's? These are the questions that help define the *vision* of your homes and your community. Once a customer has captured your vision, then you are in a position to sell your features and benefits with greater impact. You have given your homes a ***unique sense of purpose*** in the customer's mind.

It is important that customers hear your concept before they see your homes, so they will see your homes from your point of view. If they don't, they may be seeing them from the point of view of the last salesperson they talked to, or the last friend who gave them advice, or from some misconception they brought along with them.

Concepts appeal to customers because they add a dimension of intelligence to your product. Understanding your concept helps customers realize that serious thought went into every decision your company made throughout the product design phase. It makes them realize there were no accidents. Everything you did was for a purpose. This idea can be recalled when overcoming objections.

There are many ways to explain a concept. Here are a few examples.

- *"Let me give you an overview of what we're offering here. When we designed these homes, our goal was to put more space than you would expect in the rooms where you spend most of your time."*

- *"We've sold 26 homes here so far. One of the reasons people choose these homes is they like the fact that we include features they didn't expect to see in this price range."*
- *"When we bought this land we saw an unusual opportunity to offer a better combination of home and lot for the money than you'd find at other places. People here don't have to give up one to get the other. That's unusual for this location."*
- *"What makes these townhomes special is that they have a lot of the feeling you would expect in a single family home."*
- *"The reason these homes have been so popular is they offer the best kitchen/family room of any home in our price range."*
- *"These homes are built on smaller lots because if a large lot isn't your top priority, then you can use the money you would have wasted on a larger lot to get more home in a better location."*
- *"People tell us we offer the best value of any home around. When they say value, what they mean is…[insert your project's unique definition of value]."*
- *"A lot of people choose these homes because of the approach we take to architecture. We're known for more sophisticated designs than other builders in our price range."*
- *"Our homes cost a little more, but we give a lot more. People tell us we offer a better total package for the money. We focused on the exteriors and the community features as well as the floorplans. People like the fact that they're not making sacrifices here."*

If you are priced below your competitors, or are less expensive per square foot, then, of course, price can be a concept all its own.

Your selling message is only a minute or two of your total selling process. Think of it as a springboard for the rest of your presentation. It does not take the place of identifying and fulfilling the customer's needs. It complements need fulfillment by helping to **retrain the customer's thought process** so they can understand how you are not only meeting their needs, but also offering them a superior home and value. You may occasionally be fortunate enough to offer a home that perfectly matches the customer's ideal. But when this is not the case (which is most if the time), the competitive aspect of selling comes into play. Your selling message (or concept statement or positioning statement) is what helps you establish your competitive advantage as early as possible.

All of the other elements of selling (establishing rapport, creating involvement, fulfilling needs, demonstrating features and benefits) are still as important as ever. But your basic selling message helps you shape the customer's thought process so that all of your other selling tools will have greater impact.

Creating Value

For the next two chapters we are going to take a detour from the selling process to discuss two kinds of special challenges: *selling value* and *handling objections*. Now that we have defined a *success mentality* and discussed how to get the sale started, the next step is to make sure you are confident in selling your value and handling objections before we discuss the rest of the selling process. Once you have completed the greeting stage of the sale, the challenges of value and objections can begin to invade the selling process at any moment. We will discuss ways to handle these challenges with strength as well as confidence. Selling value and handling objections require not only skills and techniques, but also a mentality for success.

This chapter will explore ways to sell the unique value of your homes, as well as ways to handle pricing challenges such as discounting and negotiation. Since I will discuss a number of approaches to a variety of situations, some of my suggestions may not be relevant to your situation or your individual selling style. However, the primary purpose of the examples we will discuss is to create a total way of thinking that will enable you to sell with confidence and strength.

When buyers are trying to decide which home to choose, one of the most perplexing parts of their decision is figuring out whether their favorite home is also the best home for the money. They are trying to balance the fulfillment of their needs and desires with the assurance that they are making a sound investment.

Value is a far-reaching concept. It not only includes getting the best home for the money, but also getting the best possible price. If customers believe they are getting the best home for the money, and then the best price they can get on that home, they are more motivated to overcome other fears, concerns or objections they may have.

One way customers question value relates strictly to price. Why does your home cost as much as it does? Another concern they have relates to negotiating. If you do not discount or negotiate as much as a competitor does, customers may believe that the competitor is offering a better value. We will look at each of these challenges and discuss ways to overcome them.

DEFINING VALUE FOR CUSTOMERS

Buyers are always looking for the "best value." The problem is that they are not always sure what value in a new home really means. Some customers believe it can be measured solely in terms of price per square foot. The problem with this notion is that it fails to take into account the features included in the home, the home site, the location or the community amenities.

Many customers seem to need the reassurance that they are getting the best deal in the market before they can make a final buying decision. The problem is that in our business it can be hard for a customer to figure out what the "best deal" really is.

Every builder defines value in a slightly different way. This is what makes choosing the "best deal" so confusing. In their confusion, some customers oversimplify the concept of value by reducing it to overall price (or price per square foot), or the size of the discount. If you are offering the lowest price, or the lowest price per square foot, or the biggest discount, then, of course, you need to sell that advantage. But if your company defines value in some other way, then customers need to understand this. They need to see that your company really is focused on providing value, and that, as a salesperson, you truly believe in the unique value advantages that your homes provide.

Other than square footage, what value advantage do you believe your homes offer? Could it be more features included in the base price? A more convenient or prestigious location? Larger home sites (or home sites that are superior in some other way)? More open space? A better amenity package? Better quality? Better architecture? All of these features offer genuine value, and they all cost money to provide. If you are not the least expensive home in the market, then you will need to sell the value of your ***total package*** – a better total combination of features than your competition is offering.

Suppose a customer says to you, "The builder down the street offers a lower price than you do." You can answer by saying, *"Yes, I know they do. We're never the cheapest home in the market. That's not our goal, and it's not what we're known for. When people choose us, it's because they feel we offer a better total value. Our goal is always to offer the best home for the money, which is a lot different than offering the lowest price. When I say 'best home for the money,' what I mean is _____."* This is where you would explain your unique value benefits – your definition of value. You want to show your customers that your company is sincerely committed to the concept of value, and that you personally believe in their concept.

SELLING "ADJUSTED PRICE PER SQUARE FOOT"

Selling the value of a higher price per square foot is a challenge for many salespeople. We know there is a group of buyers for whom price per square foot is a top priority, just as there is a group for whom getting the biggest discount is a top priority. If you are selling a less expensive home per square foot than your competition, then you certainly have a valid market position, and a market that is searching for exactly what you are offering. On the other hand, if your price per square foot is higher, be sure you can make a credible statement for why.

When customers are defining value in terms of price per square foot, help them redefine value in terms of **adjusted price per square foot**. If customers tell you they can get more square footage for their money somewhere else, you could respond with the following approach.

"Shopping price per square foot is certainly important. It's one way to measure value. But if you're going to measure value that way, then you should do it the way an appraiser does. They're the experts at comparing value. When they do a competitive market analysis, they use the price and square footage as a starting point. Then they make what they call 'adjustments' in order to establish the true value. The reason they do this is they realize that comparing price per square foot alone can be misleading, and can result in a false appraisal of value.

"They adjust the price of each home they are comparing to account for lot size, location, amenities, and the specific features that each home includes. The result is what they call the 'adjusted price per square foot.' That is the really important number when you're comparing value.

"We do the same kind of competitive market analysis when we shop our competition and set our prices. That is how we know whether or not we are really competitive. If you'd like, I can show you how it works."

If you want to go a step farther, you can add the following point.

"Price per square foot by itself is meaningless. Anyone can produce a cheaper home per square foot. All they have to do is put less in the home, and put it on a less expensive lot in a less desirable location, and they have a lower price per square foot. But it doesn't mean they have a better value."

Another point you could make is this:

"Since every builder defines value a little differently, comparing the adjusted price per square foot is the equalizer. The more people understand how value works from an appraiser's point of view, they better they like our value."

Your goal is to arouse the customer's curiosity as to how this approach to value really works, so they will actually want you to make the points you need to make, and then be receptive to those points. While you do not want to be too long-winded in your explanation, you need to be thorough enough to enable the skeptical customer to really understand. You also want to show that you and your company understand the true meaning of value better than your competition, are more committed to offering it, and have a more sophisticated approach to providing it.

OBJECTIVE VALUE vs. SUBJECTIVE VALUE

Value is more than just numbers. While value includes an ***objective*** element (which is primarily numbers), it also includes a ***subjective*** element. Objective value can be impartially measured, such as price per square foot or adjusted price per square foot as discussed above. However, other aspects of value are less tangible, such as the builder's reputation, the architecture, the floor plan, the community, or simply the fact that some customers will say, "This home is just right for me; I feel like this was meant to be."

Different customers define value in different ways, depending upon their particular needs. Learning the needs of your customers will help you sell the "subjective" value of your homes. Knowing the tangible advantages you have over your competition will help you sell your "objective" value.

For selling your objective value, there is another way of looking at the concept of "adjusted price per square foot." Help your customers stay focused on the value of your ***total package***. Customers need to be comparing total packages, not just prices. While this is an obvious principle to us, it is often difficult for customers to grasp. Sometimes you must attribute specific values to each of the advantages you offer, so customers can keep track of your advantages while they compare prices. For example, you could explain your higher price to a customer like this:

"I realize we are $20,000 more than they are, and we have studied them very carefully. We know we have to offer a better value for people to choose our homes. Let me show you how we compare ourselves to them when we do a pricing analysis. First of all, our home is 100 square feet larger. That's worth about $10,000. We have a walkout basement, while theirs is buried. A walkout basement is generally worth about $5000 more in this market. A brick front is worth another $8000. Our better amenity package is worth at least $5000. Our location is worth at least $5000 more than theirs. So we really do believe we're giving you at least $33,000 more in value for $20,000 more in price. They have the lower price, but we have the better price. Our goal is not to offer the cheapest home in the market, but to offer the best home for the money. If our homes weren't worth the price, people wouldn't be buying them."

For many customers, the salesperson who wins them will be the one who can define his or her value in the most convincing terms. To sell value, you must make sure the customer understands your company's definition of value at your community. Theoretically, every builder defines value in a slightly different way.

It is important to explain to the customer early in the process what your unique definition of value is. They should hear this before they even see your homes, so they can see your homes from your point of view. We discussed this idea earlier with "concept selling." Part of controlling the sale is making sure your customers are evaluating your homes from your standpoint, not from the standpoint of the last sales presentation they heard, which may have been taking an entirely different approach to value than the one you have taken.

As you get to know your customers and their needs better, you will have opportunities to tailor your definition of value to their needs. But there is still a part of your definition that needs to come out right away, because that is why you built your homes in the first place. Taking this position before you have learned their needs is not as risky as it might seem, especially if you are targeting a particular market.

Of course, there will be times when customers immediately reveal information that allows you to tailor your presentation to their definition of value. These are the times when you are offering exactly what they are looking for at a price they can accept. Whenever you are fortunate enough to have this situation, follow it in the direction that seems most appropriate. But if you have a customer who is less explicit, or whose ideal is a little farther away from what you are offering, then you have an opportunity to present your definition of value and show why it is best.

Even if you seem to be at a disadvantage in terms of objective value, don't give up hope that subjective value could still win you the sale. If you can 1) create a better experience for your customers during their visit to your community than other salespeople provide, 2) get your customers to like you, your home and your builder well enough, and 3) show that you are fulfilling their individual needs better than anyone else, they may decide to spend a little more because they believe you are worth it – or because they believe they are worth it.

COMPETING AGAINST A LOWER PRICE

Customers will frequently want your superior home at your competitor's lower price. What else is new? You can't blame them for trying. However, you need to get them back on track. In this situation we sometimes get so caught up in trying to justify our value we forget that the customer has already decided we have the better home. We have already sold them on our value. Now it's time to let them sell us. Here is an example of how to do this.

"I would love to be able to sell you my home for their price, but I can't. Then again, neither can they. Let me ask you this: if both

homes were the same price, which would you choose?"

If the customer says they would choose the competitor's, what are they doing back at your community? However, if they say they would choose yours, you can ask why, and then respond to their answer by saying, *"That's why we're more."* The benefit of this approach is that it allows your customers to put into their words why they think your homes are better. You can use their own testimony to explain why your homes cost a little more, but still offer the best value.

There's nothing wrong with admitting you spend a little more money to build a better home. *"We do put more money into our homes, but we spend that money very well. Our approach is that for just a few dollars a week more you can get a better quality of life."* People make this decision in other areas of their lives. They will gladly spend $100 a month more to get a nicer car, or $50 a month more to drink bottled water. Why would they not do the same for their home? Sometimes we don't have to get them to change the way they think; we only have to remind them of the way they already think.

Help them remember the big picture:

"When you make a decision this important, be sure to think long term. I know it seems like a victory to get the lowest price. But what you are really looking for is the best quality of life you can get for the money. You need to think about the price of your home on a day-to-day basis, because that's the way you enjoy it. A $10,000 price difference is a couple of dollars a day. People spend more money than that on bottled water, beer, snacks, cable tv, any number of things that are all less important than the home they live in. Your home will have a greater effect on your quality of life than the cost per day of the price difference. You owe it to yourself to live in the home you want."

MAINTAINING CONTROL IN NEGOTIATION

When the market slows down, some builders negotiate their prices more than others. If your company does not negotiate or give discounts, and you are competing against other builders who do, then you need to be able to sell your position with credibility. You want to stand tall and not appear defensive. You want to be confident in your own mind that you are not vulnerable just because you don't discount.

MAINTAINING STRENGTH AGAINST DISCOUNTS

For many customers the issue of discounting gets tangled up with the issue of value. Sometimes you need to help customers understand that discounting and value are two different topics. A customer may ask for a discount (or a bigger one than you already offer) on the grounds that you should be willing to match a competitor's discount if you really want to make a sale. Making this kind of request in an industry where everyone's product is different proves they need your help in reasoning through the idea of discounting.

While your competition is using discounts as their position of strength, you want to be able to offer the fact that you do not discount as yours. One approach you could take is this:

"I know that some of the other builders in this area give discounts. They believe discounts make an excellent closing tool, and they're right. By giving up discounts, we lose a closing tool. On the other hand, in order to be able to use discounts as a closing tool, you have to inflate your original price. That just doesn't make sense to us. We want to be able to offer the best price we can to everyone as soon as they walk in the door. We don't want to risk losing customers because our ads, Realtor flyers and price lists all show inflated prices. We believe it makes more sense to take our best shot as quickly as we can. We also believe it protects our credibility. New homes are different from resales, because you wind up having your buyers as neighbors. When they start talking to each other about the deals they got, we don't want to have to run for cover. We want everyone to realize we told them the truth."

Another approach could be this:

"I know it's confusing to go from one place to another and have everyone present you with a different pricing strategy. Just remember, that's what discounting is – a pricing strategy. A discount is not the same as a deal, and it's not the same as a value. I can't give you the lowest price in the market, or the biggest discount. What I can give you is the best home for the money."

You may have situations in which it makes sense to give the following explanation:

"Everyone in our industry sells a home for as much as they possibly can. They just approach it in different ways. But remember, if someone is giving you $10,000 off the price, they're only doing it because they know if they offered $9000 off they couldn't sell the home. There's a saying in our industry that the best deal is often on the worst home."

You could simply ask the customer, *"Why do you think they have to offer such big discounts?"* or, *"With them offering such a great deal, why haven't you bought there already?"*

Sometimes customers seem to get so caught up in getting a bigger discount that they lose sight of the bigger picture. Here is a way to try to help them regain their perspective.

"I wish I could give you a bigger discount, and if I could I would. I earn my living by making sales, so the last thing I will ever do is let a customer get out the door without giving them my best price.

"What you need to do is decide which home you like best, and whether you can afford the home, and then base your decision on that, not on the size of the discount. If you buy a home based on the size of the discount, you'll never forgive yourself. As soon as you move into the home, the discount won't matter any more. What will matter is whether you got the home you wanted."

Another idea to consider is this:

"When builders negotiate their price, they are telling you they don't believe in their value. When they don't negotiate, they're

telling you they do believe in their value."

When a customer seems stuck on the notion of getting the best deal, sometimes the problem is that they have not figured out what that means. You may want to ask them how they expect you to prove you are giving them the best deal. Get them to tell you how to sell them a home.

"I appreciate the fact that you want the best deal possible. We want to be the ones to give you the best deal and earn your business. Let me ask you this: How will you know when you get the best deal?"

Throw the ball back into their court, and let them tell you how they measure value. Then you can provide the appropriate response in the terms that are most relevant to them.

MAINTAINING STRENGTH WITH DISCOUNTS

If you do negotiate or offer discounts, you still need to maintain your position of strength. One way to protect your position is to follow this principle: *A concession that is earned has more value than a concession that is given.* Our position of strength deteriorates when we begin giving things away. This is especially true if we give away everything we can offer before a customer has even shown interest in a particular home. We are admitting to the buyer that we are doubting our own value, and we are challenging the buyer to find out how much we doubt it. Therefore, if we want to protect our position of strength, we should never "give" anything away. We should provide opportunities for customers to earn our concessions.

For example, if you are offering incentives for prompt closing on inventory homes, you could take one of two approaches. You could say, "Buy our home today and we'll give you $6000 off." The problem with this approach is that it makes you look desperate while it raises doubt about the true value of your homes. The other approach would be:

"We have a completed home that we are prepared to carry for

four months until it is occupied. A home in this price range costs $2000 a month to carry. If you can buy this home and close in 30 days, you will be saving us $6000 in carrying costs, and we can pass that on to you. We don't have any negotiating room built into our price, but you can keep any money you can save us."

This approach protects the integrity of your value, and therefore protects your position of strength in negotiation. It also continues to protect your position between contract and closing. At the same time, it allows the buyer to achieve the ultimate negotiating triumph – earning a concession by legitimate means that another buyer might not have been able to earn.

Saved carrying costs is one way customers can "earn" their concession. Another way to justify "compensating" customers is that with a finished home they are accepting selections someone else made, some of which they might not have chosen for themselves. You could offer pre-selected options at a discount without eroding the basic value of your home.

A true negotiation is a "win-win" situation in which the primary needs of everyone are being met. All serious parties to a negotiation realize they may have to give up something of lesser value to them in order to acquire something of greater value. When this spirit of give and take cannot be achieved, it means the selling process never really reached the stage of legitimate negotiation. It simply got stuck at the level of customer demands.

Having said all of this, if the position your company has chosen is to give the biggest discounts in the marketplace, then there is no reason to be coy about it. Go ahead and tell it like it is. You are a very motivated seller because _____. Let your customers feel fortunate that they are in the right place at the right time, with an extraordinary opportunity being offered to them.

Prepackaged incentives (such as those given for using a preferred lender, or for buying in an earlier section) are a different situation. These are not discounts or negotiable incentives. They are part of your basic pricing package that is offered to everyone. They can therefore be discussed as soon as the information is relevant to the customer's ability to buy.

When prices are simply reduced – because the market has deteriorated, or because it has been determined that your previous prices were too high – that is a different topic than the strategies for selling value that are being discussed here.

MAINTAINING STRENGTH AGAINST UNREASONABLE OFFERS

When a customer makes an offer so low that you know it will either be countered or totally rejected, the challenge becomes preparing the customer without jeopardizing their dignity. You also want to get some idea of whether their intentions are sincere before you submit the offer. Here are several approaches you can take with a customer in this type of situation.

- *"I realize that you're offering low because you want to make sure you know where the bottom is, but please understand that if this offer is countered at all it will be countered much higher than this."*

- *"I have one major concern about submitting this offer, and that is that if we can't meet you half way you might think of it as an insult. After all the work we've both put into this, I don't want to run the risk of making you angry. I've really enjoyed working with you, and I'd like to have you as a customer."*

- *"I know from past experience that there's no way we can accept this offer, because we've turned down better offers than this already. I know we can't afford to sell the home at this price, and my boss will just tell me to try to sell it again tomorrow."*

- *"I have several people I could call right now that would offer more for this home, and my company knows that. So I know I don't have a chance of getting this accepted. Is it worth our while for me to even try for a counter?"*

- *"You're making your lowest offer on our best home and site. If getting a deal really is a priority for you, perhaps we could look at a different one."*

- *"We don't usually get offers this low. It makes me concerned whether you're really happy with this home, because that's the important question."*

One final thought on negotiation, especially in the case of unreasonable offers, is that sometimes it is okay to let the customer walk away. Walking away and not being chased may be the only way the customer will be convinced that your value is real. If they want your home and can afford it, they'll be back, and your position will be stronger.

CHAPTER

Handling Objections

For most customers, objections are a natural part of their decision-making process. They are not necessarily obstacles to completing the sale. Sometimes objections actually help customers to move forward.

In this chapter I will discuss how a success mentality relates to handling objections. I will discuss a few general principles for handling objections, and then explore a number of specific examples of the kinds of objections that frequently arise.

I use the phrase "handling objections" as opposed to "overcoming objections" because objections do not always have to be overcome in order for a sale to be made. We have all made sales where we failed to overcome at least one objection. The customer bought the home anyway. Likewise, we have had situations where we succeeded in overcoming all the objections and the customer still did not buy. Part of our ability to handle objections involves having the right perspective for them.

THINK OF OBJECTIONS AS FRIENDS, NOT ENEMIES

Why don't objections always have to be overcome? Because *people are willing to tolerate imperfections in things they really want*. Another way of saying this is *people will accept what they don't want in order to get what they do want*. These principles relate not only to material possessions, but also to human relationships. We tolerate an unfavorable characteristic in a friend or loved one that we find loathsome in someone we dislike otherwise. The same principles apply to buying a home. Most people realize they will never find the perfect home. Once they find the one that best suits their needs, they will accept shortcomings as long as the home is the best alternative of anything available, better than where they live now, and within their price range.

An objection is *an unfavorable comparison in the customer's mind between your home and their ideal*. But when the time comes for them to make their final decision, the customer's ideal will no longer be an option. They will have to decide which of the available choices will provide the best total quality of life. No one else's home will match their ideal either, and their current home isn't matching it. At some point every customer makes compromises in order to justify their decision to buy the home they want the most.

Once you understand the vital role that objections play in the process through which customers make their final buying decision, you begin to think of objections as friends, not enemies. Consider them as feedback instead of obstacles. As you show your homes, you always hope for positive responses. But negative responses can be just as good if you approach them with a positive attitude. Expect objections. It is difficult for many people to make an investment this large without raising some. They may even feel foolish if they do not raise any.

UNDERSTAND THE REASON BEHIND THE OBJECTION

Why do customers raise objections? Here are five possible reasons.

1. They're scared. When you believe the objection is more an

expression of fear than of criticism, try to get them to open up about their fears. Ask them, *"How are you feeling about the whole idea of buying a home?"* Or tell them anecdotes about positive experiences of other people who have bought from you and been glad they did.

2. They have not yet figured out exactly what they want. In this case, use their objections to determine their real needs, and then find ways to fulfill those needs.

3. They want to be sure they are making the right decision – one they will not regret later. This is a good thing. These customers are earnest, but cautious. Here the keys are patience and sensitivity – showing customers that you care for them, and will continue to care. Show them that you take their concerns seriously, and talk through those concerns until they feel comfortable with you, and with the situation as a whole.

4. They raise objections because of psychological needs, such as the need for attention. Occasionally customers will raise objections more to feel important than to resolve specific issues. There is nothing wrong with indulging this need, as long as you can keep the sale on track as you address their concerns. If customers are raising one objection after another just to derail the process, they may have more psychological baggage than you can carry. When dealing with these kinds of objections, the key is to see whether the customers are willing to move forward with their decisions. If they are, then they are entitled to the extra attention they may need. If they are unwilling to make decisions, and are simply raising objections as a smoke screen to avoid those decisions, we are no longer dealing the issue of handling objections. We are talking about a customer who is not a serious prospect. They may simply be suffering from "pretender syndrome."

5. They don't want your home. Statistically, most customers who visit your community will not buy a home from you.

When customers raise objections because your homes are simply not what they are looking for, there may be a slight chance that you can get them to rethink their priorities by showing them why so many other people choose your homes. But if that fails, it is best to just let go and not allow their objections to discourage you. Your next chance is not far away.

CHOOSE YOUR BATTLES

When handling objections, you are trying to resolve your customers' concerns as best you can. But you also need to find out where you really stand. Is the objection merely a smoke screen, or is the customer really interested? You want to give them the answers they need to resolve their objections, but you want them to stay focused on the big picture as well. You hope to spend as little time as possible fighting battles you cannot win, or that don't matter.

When an objection is easy to resolve, the most sensible approach is simply to resolve it and move on. More difficult objections may require a different approach. If you cannot resolve the objection immediately, you might need to put it on hold while you try to evaluate the bigger picture. For example, you could say:

- *"How do you like the home other than that?"*
- *"How important is this? Is it a priority?"*
- *"Hold on to that thought, and let's see what you think of the rest of the home. Then we can talk about the issue you just brought up."*

If the objection is a "deal killer," and there is nothing you can do to resolve it, then you need to know that. Sometimes an objection really does mean, "I will not accept this home, no matter what you say."

Most of the time, if customers are seriously considering your home, an objection means they are sincerely questioning an issue and want to talk it through. They are saying, "I'm concerned about this. Tell me why I shouldn't be." They may like your home better than anything else they have seen, but need reassurance that they will be making the right decision by purchasing it. Or they simply might not have decided what they want yet, and need to put their questions on the table in the form of concerns or objections.

HAVE A PLAN FOR ADDRESSING OBJECTIONS

What is the best way to address an objection?

1. Make sure you understand the objection.

If it seems confusing or ambiguous, clarify it with the customer before you try to address it.

2. Show respect for the objection as well as for the customer.

As long as the customer's sense of dignity remains intact, you'll have a much better chance of overcoming the objection, or at least helping them to accept it. Make sure they see that you are taking them and their objection seriously.

3. Explain why you did it the way you did.

Objections can often be addressed from a simple, common sense perspective. There are no accidents. Every decision your company makes has a reason behind it. You could have done it the way the objecting customer suggested. Why did you choose to do it differently? Why have so many other customers preferred your way?

The customer needs to hear your side of the story. *"We considered doing it the way you described, but here's why we did it this way instead…"*

Customers also need to hear third party endorsements. *"A lot of folks told us they prefer it this way because..."*

Your goal is not to argue with the customer, but to introduce them to another viewpoint. Let them see your home from your perspective and from the perspective of others who have bought. This way you can at least give them a reason to accept the objection if they like everything else about the home better than the other alternatives that are available.

4. Help customers rethink their needs.

Customers walk into your sales office with certain needs, wants and preconceptions. We know that one of the most important objectives in new home sales is to identify the customer's needs and then fulfill them. However, sometimes fulfilling needs involves helping customers re-evaluate their needs, especially when they are raising objections to a home they are seriously interested in buying. Customers often wind up buying a home that is different from what they originally said they wanted, just as they wind up buying a home for 30-day completion when they originally came in planning to buy "in about a year." *Customers start out with a plan, and then change their plan when they find a home they want.*

In designing your homes you have already identified certain needs you want to fulfill. Sometimes in order to fulfill a need you must create the need in the customer's mind. In other words, make the customer aware that the need exists. You can begin to increase the customer's awareness of certain needs by showing how you have fulfilled the needs of others like them.

5. Compare the objection favorably to situations the customer already considers acceptable.

Explain how homes backing up to a road or school or power line offer more of a feeling of space and privacy than the typical situation of backing up to another home. Show how the in-ground basement offers more privacy or a flatter yard than a walkout basement.

6. Explain how customers can benefit from tradeoffs.

Show how you have been able to offer the largest family room in your price range by taking space out of the seldom-used living room or dining room. Explain to the parents of two children how you offer a better master bedroom suite by putting less space in bedroom #4, which they will not use as a full-time bedroom anyway. Let them see how you have thought through the entire situation to offer the best of what is most important.

7. Keep customers focused on the total package.

Customers will usually raise objections to your homes one feature at a time. Yet their real choice is between your total package and all of the other total packages in the real world. Customers are not able to mix and match the best of every alternative. It is hard for most customers to stay focused on the total package. They want the best of everything they have seen combined into one home for the lowest price. The reality, however, is that they have one of three options:

1. They can buy your total package.

2. They can buy someone else's total package.

3. They can remain in the total package where they currently live.

Help your customers maintain their awareness of the big picture. Keep them focused on comparing your total home with other total homes that are available for the price.

8. Determine if the objection is a bluff.

You may have occasions where you cannot go any farther with a sale until you can resolve a certain objection, and you cannot resolve the objection without making some sort of change that requires the builder's approval. If you feel that the builder may prefer to make the change rather than lose the sale, you could ask the customer, *"If I could solve this problem, would this be the home for you?"* Whether your company is able to make the change or not, at least it brings the true importance of the objection out in the open. It will flush out the smoke-screener who is just wasting your time by saying, "If you could do what I already know you can't do, I would buy your home."

DECIDE WHEN YOU WILL ADDRESS CHRONIC OBJECTIONS

Most of the time you do not want to address a potential objection until a customer brings it up. However, there are exceptions to this rule. Sometimes you know an objection is coming. It comes up almost every time. Now you have a judgment call. Is the objection an issue that everyone raises and then gets over, or is it a "stopper?" If it is the former, then there is usually no reason to bring it up in advance. Just have your answer prepared for when it arises. But if it is the kind of objection that could stall your momentum by deflating the customer's enthusiasm, then it is better to have a way of addressing it in advance to test the water. I call this **removing the "yikes" factor**. Unpleasant surprises are the enemy of momentum. You can remove the yikes factor by describing the home in advance in a positive way, while including the potential concern in as favorable a context as possible. This gives the customer a chance to adjust to the idea of the issue before they see it, instead of being shocked when they get there. After describing the home, including the objection, you can then ask if they want to see it. If they say yes, they have already taken the first step toward accepting the objection.

Naturally, you never want to appear defensive about a potential objection, especially when it may not even be an objection for that customer. However, you should consider addressing a potential objection proactively by explaining the situation merely as information (and not necessarily as a problem), when you believe that any of the following may be true:

1. Every customer will react negatively to the issue when they see it.
2. The issue will deflate your momentum just as it is reaching its peak.
3. You will put your own credibility at risk if you do not bring it up.

SOMETIMES YOU HAVE TO SAY "NO"

From time to time, customers make requests that you are unable to accommodate. Whether it is a discount you cannot give, or the extension of a closing date, or a custom change that is greater than your system is designed to provide, you have to tell the customer "no." It is important not to feel intimidated by this situation.

Some people believe that "no" is a word that should never be spoken in sales. Unfortunately, this mindset can make us afraid to say "no" when we really need to. "No" may sometimes be the best answer you can give for advancing the sale in the long run.

There were occasions when I felt as though I lost a sale by saying "no." But then I came to realize that these were not really lost sales at all. They were simply not sales. They were customers telling us, "If your homes (or prices or systems) were different, I'd buy from you." But that happens in every business every day. It is "the sale that never was." A sale is when a customer pays the price you need for the product you provide, the way you provide it.

When you lose a sale because you have to say "no" to a special request, don't let it frustrate you, especially if you believe you did the best you could to explain your answer.

The two most important elements in saying "no" are:

1. A respectful demeanor that shows genuine regard for the customer's request.
2. An intelligent explanation that conveys the purpose and

benefits of your approach, and a strong belief in that approach.

If you provide these two elements with your answer, and the customer does not buy your home, just try again with the next customer. If you get frustrated, it will only erode your confidence in yourself, your homes and your company.

Most of the time, if customers like your home better than anything else they have seen for the money, and can afford it, and are sincere about buying a new home, you will not lose a sale by saying "no" to a special request. The reason is that when customers look at your home, they usually have three options:

1. Buy your home the way you provide it.

2. Buy someone else's home the way they provide it.

3. Stay in their current home.

If you believe their interest in your home is serious enough that they would buy it, then they have presumably eliminated options 2 and 3. (If they have not yet eliminated those two options, then they are probably not yet at the point where they are ready to buy, no matter what your answer is.) The customer is now asking to introduce a fourth option – to buy your home the way they want it. Once they put that option on the table, the longer it stays there unresolved, the harder it becomes to get them to make a final decision. You need to take that fourth option back off the table, so the customer still has the same three options they always had.

Most of your sincere customers, if they like your home well enough to make the special request in the first place, have reached the point where your home was already their first choice without the special request being fulfilled. Otherwise they would be making the request of someone else. (The exception is the case of the extreme "control freak," and then we are talking about a whole new set of problems anyway. If controlling the process is more important to the customer than getting their first choice home, you may have to be prepared to lose that customer, and then be at peace with it.)

Often when customers make a special request, all they really want is an answer and an explanation. They did not really expect the request to be fulfilled, even though they may protest briefly. Other times they will walk away disappointed, and then get over it and come back. But sometimes they will not come back. You cannot be all things to all people. You can only do the best job possible of explaining who you are and why.

Do not allow saying "no" to become more complicated than it really is. Sometimes we make the mistake of saying, "I'm sorry, it's impossible." Yet the customer believes it is not really impossible, but merely inconvenient. They look at it from the standpoint, "I know it's possible, and I'm willing to pay for it. So the only reason you would not do it is that you don't care about me." It is not unreasonable for customers to think this way when they don't fully understand how the construction process works. So you should not tell the customer it's impossible, and you should not tell them, "You don't really want that. It will be hard to resell." You run the risk of insulting their taste or intelligence.

You are better off simply explaining to them, *"I'm afraid we're just not set up that way. The way our system works is* _____ [Explain those parts of your system that are relevant to their concern]. *And the reason we do it that way is* _____ [Explain the benefits of your system and the thought process behind it]. *It's the system that has made us successful and earned us our good reputation. If our system were set up to accommodate this kind of request, then we would run the risk of* _____ [Explain the disruption that could occur], *and then we would not be able to* _____ [Explain the benefits to customers that could be lost]." While this kind of answer may disappoint the customer, it is respectful, thoughtful, knowledgeable and honest.

The next step is to make sure that you, your construction team and your managers are all consistent in the way you answer the request, in case the customer decides to pursue it. If they get different stories from different employees, the relationship begins to spiral downward.

Up to this point we have discussed general principles for developing a success mentality for handling objections. Now we will look at ways to apply these principles to specific objections.

HOMES THAT BACK UP TO A ROAD

So many customers object to a home that backs up to a road, and yet so many buy them. The problem with roads is that they are rarely on a customer's wish list. Our lives would be so much easier if customers said, "We're looking for a home that backs up to a road. Can you help us?" Most customers have not yet created a place in their brain to put a road that runs behind a home. Your goal is to help them create that place. A road is the kind of concern where, once customers think it all the way through, they frequently decide that it is not really such a bad situation. Some even choose it over the other alternatives that are available.

If a home backs up to an interstate highway, that is a special situation. When customers accept this situation, it may be because the distance to the highway is great enough, or a sound wall is effective, or special soundproofing insulation in the home muffles the noise, or some other compensating benefit makes the highway acceptable. What I am talking about here is the typical, medium-sized, 45 mile per hour road. Let's suppose that the builder does not include privacy fencing. We will explore a line of reasoning as to why it might make sense for buyers to accept the road behind the home if they like everything else about the home well enough to buy it.

Some customers are completely closed-minded on the subject of backing up to a road. We know that having a road behind a home will eliminate a certain portion of the market. Surprisingly, at the other end of the spectrum are people who seem not to care at all about the road. To them, it is not even a factor. Here we will be talking about the buyer who is in between these two extremes – the one who says, "Tell me why I should buy a home backing up to a road."

Begin by asking the customers what their concerns are, unless you already believe their concerns are obvious. Generally the concerns involve privacy and noise. If the customers like the home otherwise, and are open-minded about what you have to say, they may want you to give a thorough explanation of why people buy homes backing to a road. In this case, begin by saying:

"When we have homes backing up to a road on the market at the same time as homes backing up to other homes, some people choose the homes with the road."

This would be an example of the principle of comparing the objection favorably to situations the customer already considers acceptable. Since customers think of backing up to another home as the norm, is there a way we can make the road look more desirable than the norm? You could continue by saying,

"One reason is that the road offers more of a feeling of space, because it's more open than backing up to another home."

People sometimes wonder about the privacy of backing to a road. Naturally, if there is a privacy fence at the back of the lot, then this issue goes away. But if it there is no fence, you could say:

"When people are driving by in their cars, they have to keep their eyes on the road. They can't pay attention to you the way people living behind you can. A lot of folks who back up to a road feel that their situation is actually more private than backing up to another home.

"Then there is the question of the sound of the cars going by. That is something you'll have to decide for yourself. But there has been a lot of research done on this topic that explains why builders keep building homes backing to roads, and why buyers keep buying them. When people who live in homes backing up to this kind of road are asked what it's like, one answer comes up again and again. People say they stopped noticing the sound after a short time. It just became a part of their lives that never bothered them again."

If you have a customer who is more analytical, or who seems to need a more detailed explanation of how this could be possible, the explanation could sound like this:

"It involves the difference between sound and noise. Sound is natural. It exists in the background. Noise is disruptive. It takes over your consciousness. We have sound all the time – heaters and air conditioners, appliances, airplanes, even lawn mowers. You never hear people complain about the sound of a lawn mower, even though it would drown out the sound of the cars from the road. When a noise is disruptive, it means that if you were having a conversation you would have to raise your voice; if you are asleep it would wake you up; if you were reading it would interrupt your train of thought. The sound of this road would be unlikely to have those effects even if you were sitting outside, or inside with the windows open. With the windows closed you may barely even notice the sound, but that's for you to decide."

You want to sound objective more than persuasive. Your goal is not to try to shove something down the customer's throat they don't want, but rather to help them find a place in their brain to put a road. You want them to make the decision that is best for them, but also to consider the possibility that a road offers more positives than negatives. Here we are talking about the principles of helping customers to rethink their needs and explaining how customers can benefit from tradeoffs. Depending on the impact of the road, you may even want to discuss the issue while you are out in the back yard with customers. You could say:

"We've been talking for several minutes out here, and the sound of the cars hasn't interfered with our conversation or forced us to talk louder."

You could then conclude your explanation by saying:

"When folks choose a home backing to a road, they feel that the down side – the sound of cars – goes away after a short time, while the upside – openness and privacy – lasts forever. Homes backing up to this kind of road always sell, or we wouldn't keep buying the land."

SMALL HOME SITES

Your home sites may be smaller than some customers were hoping for. If customers absolutely must have a larger site in order to accommodate an important lifestyle need, they may be willing to sacrifice location or square footage in their home in order to get it. However, many customers start out wanting a larger home site merely as part of the Great American Dream. They have not yet reached the point of considering what cost or sacrifice is involved in getting a larger home site. You must bring them to the point of understanding the cost. Once again, we will use the principles discussed earlier:

1. Make sure you understand the objection.

2. Explain why you did it the way you did it.

3. Help customers rethink their needs. (Customers start out with a plan, and then change their plan when they find the home they want.)

4. Explain how customers can benefit from tradeoffs.

When customers say they want a larger home site than you offer, you could begin by asking:

"Do you have a specific plan for your lot, or did you just want as much space as possible?"

If their answer gives you reason for hope, you could continue by saying:

"For the last thirty years, the trend toward smaller home sites has been largely consumer driven. Many people who start out wanting a larger site wind up changing their minds. And many people who chose a larger site with their previous home would choose a smaller site if they had it to do over. The reason is that if a large site is not an absolute necessity, then a smaller site allows you to get more home in a better location for less money."

It's a simple and obvious principle, but for many customers it takes awhile for the full impact of it to sink in. They have to visit several places with different lot sizes to realize the sacrifices they will make in order to get a larger lot. If you need to say more, you could continue:

"It winds up being a quality of life issue. Instead of spending extra money for a larger site, you get more space and better features in your home. For many people, a larger site requires more maintenance than it provides enjoyment. An 8000 square foot site gives you pretty much the same lifestyle as a 10,000 square foot site. But, for the same price, the 8000 square foot site allows you to have about 300 more square feet of living space in your home, which really does make a difference in the way you live every day."

Naturally, these numbers would vary with the location, but it may be worth seeing what the correlation is in your area. You could then conclude by saying:

"Like many builders, we are building more of our homes on smaller sites because they are easier to sell. The reason is that there is a larger market for the total package of value and location we can offer with a smaller site. Larger sites are getting harder and harder to sell, even though many people start out wanting one."

SLOPING HOME SITES

A home site that slopes up or down in the back may be an example of a situation you should describe to customers in advance so they will not be shocked when they get there. We talked earlier about removing the "yikes factor." As with a road, a sloping lot is not usually something that is on a customer's wish list. Yet they often choose it once they find a place in their brain to put it. You may feel you need to address the issue up front so customers can warm up to the concept before they see the lot. Here is one approach for a lot that slopes up in the back:

"One site I would like to show you has great aesthetics, but not a flat back yard. Do you need a lot of flat space?...The back yard goes out flat for about 20 feet, and then slopes up to the site behind it. What makes this lot nice is that it gives you more of

a feeling of distance and privacy from the home behind than if the yard were flat. It also gives the lot a nicer look. Flat yards always have that average look, while topography adds beauty. In fact, the rolling topography was one of the reasons we bought this land. We knew the community would have wonderful aesthetics when it was done. A lot of folks feel that looking out into a hill is more appealing than looking into another home at the same level. Plus, if you landscape the hill, it can create an appealing visual experience from the home as well as the patio."

You may also want to explain the drainage of the back yard in order to show customers how water from the hill will be kept away from the home through swales.

If the lot slopes down in the back to another home, explain the aesthetic benefit of sitting up higher than the home behind.

Of course, if there is no home behind, but trees or open space instead, then these become the features, with the slope adding to the aesthetics (if the hill goes up) or the view (if the hill slopes down).

CORNER HOME SITES

Some customers prefer corner home sites, while others consider them objectionable. Then there are customers who have never thought about a corner lot one way or another. As with the previous objections we have discussed, you want to help customers realize why so many other people choose corner lots. Since corner lots vary, some of the following points may not apply to every corner lot.

"Some people prefer corner home sites because they offer three yards instead of two. [The side yard may even be as large as the front or back. If this is the case, be sure to emphasize it.] There is no neighbor on one side, so it feels more open. It also has more landscaping possibilities. By sitting on a corner with

landscaping potential on the side as well as the front, it has more showcasing possibilities. For that reason, some homeowners feel that a corner site is more prestigious."

Corner lots sometimes create a negative impact on the back yard in terms of size and privacy. If this is true with your lot, wait for the customer to comment so you can see how they view the entire situation on balance. If there is no negative impact upon the back yard, then you may want to explain to the customer that this one potential pitfall of a corner lot does not apply in their case, so they are getting the best of all possible worlds.

SMALL BEDROOMS

If you are selling homes with small secondary bedrooms, you may hear objections to the size of those rooms fairly often. Occasionally you may even lose a sale because the bedrooms really are too small for a customer's desired use. See if you can justify the bedroom sizes in a way that will help your customers feel okay about accepting them.

When customers raise objections, sometimes you try to overcome the objection, while other times you help the customer accept the objection because they like everything else about the home. You might even ask the question, *"Other than the size of the secondary bedrooms, how do you like the rest of the home?"* If the bedroom sizes are a serious objection in a home they otherwise like, here are a few suggestions for helping them accept the smaller bedrooms.

Begin by explaining the thought process behind small bedrooms. After all, the small bedrooms were not an accident. They were designed into the home with a sense of purpose, just like every other room. Figure out exactly what furniture will fit into the room, and then discuss the room in terms of the furniture for which it was designed. Give the room a clear sense of purpose. Here are three examples:

1. *"This room was designed for a twin bed, a desk and a*

dresser."

2. "*This room can easily hold a double bed, a desk and a dresser, which is pretty good for a secondary bedroom in this price range. But what about your child (use a name if possible)? Will her things fit?*"

Once you have explained your approach in designing the room, move to the more important issue – will it work for the customer? Ask about their specific furniture, and try to place their furniture in the room as exactly as possible using a tape measure and their estimate of the size of furniture. They may even need to go home and measure the furniture, and then come back. The fact that a room seems small doesn't necessarily mean it won't meet their needs. You want to create a conversation in which you are discussing function, and not just dimensions. Now here is the third example.

3. "*We designed bedroom #3 for a small child, or for a study, or for a guest room. This way we could make bedroom #2 larger than average.*"

Try to provide a corresponding benefit that offers more of an advantage than the small bedroom is a liability. Another principle you can explain is this:

"*When a builder tries to create value in a home, an important design principle for making the best use of every square foot is to think through how the space will be used, and also how it will be perceived. Children view space in a bedroom differently than adults do. Adults view space in the master bedroom in terms of the space between things. Children have a different concept of space. They look at their bedroom in terms like, 'Is this my room? Does the door lock? Does my stuff fit?' They're not as concerned with the space between things as adults are. It's interesting that when an older child who has the bigger bedroom leaves home, the younger child sometimes has no interest in moving out of his room in order to move into the bigger one. That's because the bigger one just isn't his room.*"

"If you make the kids' rooms a little smaller, but still big enough to meet their needs, then you can free up more space to put into the master bedroom, where extra square footage means more. The goal in good design is to give everyone the things that are most important to them. Give the kids what the kids want, and give the adults what the adults want. And don't forget, nobody in this price range has secondary bedrooms that are much larger unless the master bedroom takes a big hit."

See if there are any other special benefits such as larger closets, or more unbroken wall space due to windows or doors that are strategically located.

Unless specific furniture or some other need rules out your bedrooms, customers may be willing to accept smaller bedrooms if:

- They understand your thought process and the purpose of your design.
- They see a corresponding benefit.
- They understand that your bedroom sizes are competitive for your price range.
- They like the home enough to own it otherwise.

OTHER SMALL ROOMS

You can handle objections to other small rooms with a similar approach to the one suggested for small bedrooms: explaining the thought process behind the decision, showing how it is a tradeoff that produces a greater benefit, and then seeing if it will work well enough for the customers in light of the total package they are getting vs. the other options that are available in the real world.

FOYERS

If you offer a foyer that is smaller than the competition, you can once again express the goal of making every square foot achieve its maximum value. Explain that the purpose behind the design of the home was to provide better value by putting more square footage into the destination areas, and less into those areas that serve as transitions to the destination areas. If a home costs $100 per square foot, does the customer really want to spend $15,000 in the foyer of a $200,000 home, and then have a smaller kitchen and family room as a result?

LIVING AND DINING ROOMS

Here the position would be that today's buyers are demanding larger family rooms and kitchens, and at the same time are using living rooms and dining rooms less than they used to. You are putting your square footage, and consequently the customer's money, into the areas where they will be rewarded with the greatest benefit in their overall quality of life.

KITCHENS

Small kitchens are a tougher objection to overcome. It may come down to finding out if the customer's dishes and appliances will fit into the cabinets and pantries, and whether the counter space is workable. The upside is that today a home with a small kitchen is usually pretty well priced, or else it is in an excellent location for the money.

FAMILY ROOMS

Since a large family room is also a high priority for so many of today's buyers, customers may initially feel that a small family room is a concession they are unwilling to make. If the small family room is next to the kitchen and open to it, you could make the point that the family/kitchen combination is laid out the way many families really live – with both areas being used as one combined living space, and with the family room television (and fireplace, if applicable) being easily enjoyed from the kitchen.

MASTER BEDROOMS

If the master bedroom is small, then overcoming it becomes largely a matter of function. Will the buyers' furniture fit? Is it practical, if not luxurious? Do they like the rest of the home well enough for the price?

LAUNDRY ROOM LOCATIONS

The first step in handling certain objections is realizing that, although customers may complain about them, they will rarely make or break a sale. The location of the laundry room is one example of such an objection. There will be some people who want the laundry room on the first floor, where the kitchen and other work areas are, while others want it upstairs, where the bedrooms are. There is no universally accepted location for the laundry room. All you can do is explain this dilemma to customers, and then justify the reasoning behind whatever laundry room location each home has.

If customers object to a laundry room that is on the main level, you could say:

"Often, the way a home lays out makes the location of the laundry room less disruptive on the main level than it would be on the second level. It is sometimes easier to find dead space near the kitchen or garage where the laundry room does not cause problems for any of the other rooms. Upstairs, there is such a premium on bedroom space. Putting the laundry room upstairs can have a negative impact on the size of bedrooms, closets and bathrooms. When a laundry room is on the main level, it's farther from the bedrooms, but it's closer to the other primary work spaces."

Some people prefer the laundry room on the first floor because it is closer to the other primary work spaces. Their objection to an upstairs laundry room is that you have to walk up and down stairs more times during the day when you are most likely to be doing your laundry. You could respond by saying:

"Since it is a two-level home, where the work areas and bedrooms are on different levels, you will wind up walking up and down stairs to do your laundry either way. At least when it's upstairs, where most of the things you are washing will wind up anyway, you won't be carrying the laundry up and down the stairs as often."

Since this is rarely an objection that causes you to lose a sale by itself, you may also want to ask:

"Other than the laundry room location, how do you like the home?"

HOMES WITH FEWER BEDROOMS

When customers raise the objection that your homes do not have enough bedrooms, the objection may be insurmountable if their need for more bedrooms is legitimate. But sometimes customers want more bedrooms simply because they think they are supposed to. They may want a four bedroom single family home when all they really need is three bedrooms, or a three bedroom townhome when all they need is two. They have no planned use for the extra bedroom, and no serious reason for wanting it. Their objection is based more on a preconception than a need.

People may have been told that homes with more bedrooms will resell more easily. This is one of those theories that many people continue to believe, even though the evidence against it is very strong. There are many hot selling three bedroom single family homes and two bedroom townhomes. There are also many homes that are designed with the flexibility to offer the choice of fewer but larger bedrooms, or more bedrooms that are smaller. While many people choose more bedrooms, there are still plenty of cases where the option of fewer, larger bedrooms outsells the option for the extra bedroom.

Naturally, if you offer homes with fewer bedrooms than the competition at the same price, you will exclude a portion of the market from choosing your homes. Families with three children often need four or more bedrooms. Some buyers also need the extra room as a study or guest room. There is nevertheless a huge market for three bedroom single family homes and two bedroom townhomes, even in the move-up price range.

Sometimes customers believe they simply have a choice between more bedrooms and less, with no difference in cost, and no other strings attached. Naturally, they would rather have more. But often there are strings attached, and explaining these strings can be the key to handling objections from customers who are in a position to go either way.

Suppose you are selling three bedroom single family homes and you are competing against communities that offer four. If the customer raises the concern about only three bedrooms, you should first ask if the fourth bedroom is a necessity. If it truly is, then that customer is not your target market. However, if customers say they want four bedrooms solely because they think it is a smarter purchase, you could answer their concern this way:

"There is an excellent market for three bedroom homes. In fact, many people choose three bedrooms over four, even if they could easily afford four. The reason is that the fourth bedroom does not come without a cost. Many buyers feel they don't need a fourth bedroom enough to pay for it, and they'd rather spend the money some other way.

"Sometimes the cost is not so much in price as it is in the size of the remaining rooms. One reason some people would rather own a $200,000 three bedroom home than a $200,000 four bedroom home is that the three bedroom home has better room sizes. If you think of the four bedroom home as a $200,000 home filled with $200,000 rooms, then you could think of a three bedroom home as a $200,000 home with several $250,000 rooms. The value is there either way. But the fewer rooms you need, the better rooms you will be able to get for your money."

This seems like an obvious concept, but customers may not have this awareness until we give it to them. As you try to identify and fulfill the needs of your customers, remember that sometimes they may not yet be fully educated as to what their needs should be, and that their needs can sometimes change as they go through the buying process.

Showing Your Homes

S howing your homes provides you with a wonderful opportunity to create a more enriching experience for your customer. It also takes your selling momentum to the next level.

Customers need your help to fully appreciate your homes. Demonstrating models offers a number of valuable opportunities in the selling process, opportunities which can be lost when customers view the models alone. The model demonstration is one of your opportunities to truly make a difference in the customer's decision of whether or not to buy a home from you.

When you are in the greeting stage, you may sometimes wonder whether to accompany your customers through the model or let them go alone. Although there will always be those customers who want to be left alone, you should still assume that serious customers want your service and knowledge unless they tell you they don't.

Some people who visit your community are not seriously in the market for a home. Others want to see the models by themselves before they see them with you. Then there are those who just need to get started by themselves, but are content to have you catch up with them after a few minutes. Ultimately it becomes a judgment call. Don't get too hung up on whether or not customers *want* you to accompany them when they see your homes. The question is not so much, "Does the customer want me to go with them?" as it is, "If I go with them, will it increase my chances of selling them a home?" and, "Can I make them glad I did go with them by the time it's over?"

Sometimes you may legitimately decide that no good purpose will be served by accompanying a customer through the models. On the other hand, you do not want to forfeit the unique selling opportunities of the model demonstration if you feel there is even the slightest chance the customer will buy a home from you. Naturally, if you use the model demonstration to annoy, pressure or browbeat customers, then your selling momentum will stall as surely as if you had let them go alone. But if you use the model demonstration to enrich your customers, then the demonstration may become the point at which you win the sale from your competition. You will impress customers with your diligence, knowledge and enthusiasm, and with your interest in them. Serious customers want serious salespeople. Those customers who are not serious will let you know when you offer your service.

A model demonstration does not have to be a contrived, scripted exhibition of features, benefits, and tie-downs. While features and benefits are an important part of model demonstration, they are not the most important part. The model demonstration gives you a chance to provide your customer with a clearer idea of what your company is about. It is also an opportunity to gain a better understanding of what your customer is about – what needs and motivations are driving them. The demonstration can be a very natural and straightforward human experience.

For example, you can start out by saying, *"Let me show you this home, and that will give me a chance to tell you a little more about us as a company, and how we do things. Also, as we're walking through, if you could tell me things you like and don't like, it will help us figure out if we have a home you might be interested in."* After all, you are not necessarily trying to sell them the model, unless that is the only kind of home you build. You are using the model as a springboard for the decision process of which home is best for them. Of course, you will be able to show your homes more effectively if you can learn a little about their needs and priorities during the greeting stage.

Your transition from the sales office to the models may be as simple as saying, *"Let me show you one of our homes."*

Some salespeople keep their brochures and price lists in the kitchen instead of the sales office. They use the sales office as a greeting area – a place to introduce themselves to their customers, ask some basic questions, and provide a general overview. But their real goal is to get out of the sales office and into the model as quickly as possible. When they get to the point where they are ready to talk about their homes in a more specific way, they say, *"I have some information on our homes in the kitchen of our model. Let's move into there. I also have some drinks and snacks if you'd like any."*

We have said that the model demonstration offers unique selling opportunities that are not available to the same degree in other stages of the selling process. Now let's take a look at what these opportunities are, and how to make the most of them.

1. Bring your selling message to life.

Your selling message (or concept) – the basic overview of why your homes are special and why people choose them – can become the theme of your model demonstration. A theme makes your demonstration more than a "Here's-the-living-room-and-here's-the-dining-room" type of house tour. It gives your demonstration a sense of purpose for you and your customer. Having a theme for your demonstration can help you build your customer's interest in what you are saying, and thereby increase your selling impact. When you show your homes to customers, you have the opportunity to bring your concept to life. During the greeting stage, your initial overview is where you say, "Here are some of the reasons people choose our homes." The model demonstration is where you say, "Let me show you what I mean."

Demonstrating the features and benefits of your homes can have more impact when those features and benefits also prove a larger point by demonstrating your superior approach to home building. Pick several features you think will have the most impact and significance. These selected features should illustrate your advantages and create customer involvement without overloading the customer with too much information. You also want to emphasize features and benefits that customers would be unlikely to notice or appreciate on their own.

The model demonstration gives you another arena for selling your builder, and for explaining how your company has achieved its success and reputation.

2. Deepen your relationships with your customers.

While the greeting sets the tone for your relationship with customers, the model demonstration can often be the time when the relationship begins to blossom. In this more casual atmosphere, you can get to know your customers better. Just as important, they can get to know you better.

You can learn more about their individual needs. Instead of talking about needs in a general way, you can now talk about them in the context of what you are selling. You can relate features and benefits to specific needs by saying, "Here's an example of what you were looking for." Customers can begin to see you as more of a counselor.

Be sure to show enthusiasm for your customers as well as your homes. You enjoy your customers and you enjoy your homes, so you enjoy going through your homes with your customers.

Taking customers through models offers special opportunities for building relationships which do not exist in any other stage of the sale. Customers get to see another dimension of your expertise. They also get to see your commitment to providing a high level of service.

3. Watch their responses, and adjust your selling strategy accordingly.

Once customers leave you to walk through the models alone, you lose control over their perception of your homes, the conclusions they draw and the decisions they make. You don't know how they are responding, and you have no opportunity to influence their responses. They might experience your homes in a much different way if you were there. Interaction with you can enrich their experience of your homes, and help them to develop their thought process in a much more positive way as the experience evolves. Interaction can also enhance their ability to make decisions about their perceptions along the way. You may even be able to turn negative perceptions into positive ones by helping them understand the purpose behind things they don't understand.

Use your demonstration to get feedback, so that you can talk about their negative responses and build momentum on the positive ones.

4. Show your expertise and that of your builder.

People want to buy from experts. Show them that you think not only like a salesperson, but also like a builder. I worked with one salesperson who set up his trip to the models by saying, *"As we go through the models, I'll explain how our homes are built."* Although explaining construction is not the most important objective of the model demonstration, this salesperson at least saw the demonstration as one valuable opportunity to show how his company was a better builder. When customers see this kind of confidence and enthusiasm, it raises their comfort level.

Show any advantages you may have in the construction, engineering, architecture or products your homes feature. Examples could include:

• The energy system.

- The floor system.
- Kitchen cabinets, appliances or layout.
- Interior design or exterior architecture. (Most salespeople do not sell architecture, which is surprising considering the business we are in. In fact, most customers rarely even hear the word.)
- Windows and doors.
- Floor coverings.
- Trim and moldings.

Many of the advantages you demonstrate can have symbolic value as well as technical value. In addition to being tangible in themselves, these benefits also make the customer feel better about the builder. They show that you not only offer construction advantages, you are a builder who is earnestly seeking to provide a better home for the money.

You could introduce special advantages by saying, *"One thing we do differently than other builders you'll visit is _____. This is one example of how we believe we build a better home for the money than anyone else in the market."*

Sometimes your item will not necessarily be unique. You may simply be the only salesperson who cared enough to point it out.

The model demonstration should not be an exercise in "feature dumping." Your goal is to point out a few items that show you are serious about building a better home. Let customers see that you really believe you are the best. Even when customers show little interest in construction or engineering, explaining a few of your homes' technical advantages can help you reassure them that they are buying from someone who cares.

5. Create involvement in the home.

Here we are talking about the emotional aspect of selling. It begins with your own enthusiasm. This is another part of "creating an enriching experience." Following are a few techniques you can use to increase the impact of your model demonstration.

Remember to keep your model demonstration interactive. When the conversation is all one-way, the demonstration becomes awkward and less productive. One way to keep the model demonstration interactive is by asking questions.

Use animation in your demonstration. Animation does not mean contrived theatrical behavior. It simply means developing certain skills that can become natural for any type of personality. Developing these skills may take commitment and practice if you do not already use them, but it does not mean you will have to change your selling personality. The following skills can be developed by anyone. They are important because they create involvement by increasing the impact of your message. As they increase your impact, they also make you and your message more memorable. Here are six skills to focus on:

- Smiling.
- Eye contact.
- Voice modulation.
- Movement and gesturing.
- Energy and enthusiasm.
- Customer involvement in demonstration activities.

Engage as many of the senses as possible in the demonstration. Throughout your demonstration customers *see* the model and *hear* you talk. Exciting the sense of *smell* with appealing aromas can make the demonstration more enjoyable and the home more attractive. Offering refreshments can engage the sense of *taste*.

When possible, encourage customers to try to *touch* items you are trying to emphasize – cabinets, faucets, appliances, handrails, etc. Touching brings an item closer emotionally as well as physically.

Bring your homes to life in the third person, the second person, or the first person. Conversation that is designed to "bring the home to life" should sound natural, not contrived. Some salespeople are very comfortable with the "Imagine yourself living here at Christmas" approach to model demonstration. Many others feel uncomfortable with it. If you are in the latter group, there are other approaches that may feel more down to earth.

- Third person approach: *"Here's what some of our homeowners have done with this space..."*

- Second person approach: *"One thing you could do with this space is..."* This approach can also be accomplished in the form of a question: *"How would you use this space if you lived here?"*

- First person approach: *"If this were my home, here's what I would do with this space..."* Another way of saying this would be, *"I'd love to have a room like this. If this were mine, here's what I'd do..."* The first person approach provides the opportunity to demonstrate your personal enthusiasm, which can be so helpful in "emotional selling." Emotional selling starts with enthusiasm and grows into involvement. As trite as it sounds, enthusiasm really is contagious. If customers can see your enthusiasm, it becomes easier for their own to be ignited.

6. Help customers make decisions.

One of the most important opportunities of the model demonstration is to get feedback that will lead to decisions. The ability to make decisions is the most genuine buying signal of all. Decisions also help you build momentum in the selling process.

The model demonstration enables you to create involvement, see the customer's responses, and adjust your strategy accordingly in order to create a *decision-making rhythm* as the demonstration progresses. In order to create a decision-making rhythm, the demonstration needs to be interactive. You always want to know what your customers are thinking, and the best way to find out is simply to ask. Feedback questions can help you keep your customers on a decision-making track. If you ask the right questions and then listen carefully enough, your customers will tell you how to sell them a home.

Examples of feedback questions include:

- *"How does this look to you?"*
- *"How do you like this home so far?"*
- *"Do you feel good about this?*
- *"Does this look like what you were talking about?"*
- *"How does this compare with what you were hoping for?"*
- *"How does this compare with other homes you've seen?"*
- *"How does this compare with your present home?"*
- [If there is another decision-maker who is not present, you could ask:] *"How do you think he/she will like it?"*
- *"How do you feel about this kitchen? Will it work for you?"*
- *"What is your favorite part of this home?"*
- *"How does this compare with the last one we looked at?"*
- *"Which one do you like best so far? What makes it your favorite?"*
- *"Is this a possibility for you?"*
- *"Is there anything about this home that doesn't work for you?"*

As you get answers to your questions and other responses to your homes, be sure to "respond to their responses." Your customers must see that their reactions are important to you. Responding with interest and enthusiasm to their reactions will encourage customers to communicate more.

Remember, you are not trying to sell them your model. You are trying to sell them one of your available homes. You are also selling the builder, eliciting responses and decisions, and making points about your homes along the way. If you have five different house types and only one model, then theoretically 80% of the time you will be using the model to set up a different floor plan. Take your other floor plans with you into the model so you can switch gears easily. You may wind up spreading out your plans on the kitchen counter of the model once you find out that the model is not the kind of home they are looking for.

We said above that the ability to make decisions is the most important buying signal of all. Throughout the model demonstration, you are trying to help your customers make smaller decisions that will lead to larger ones. The ultimate purpose of the model demonstration is to help customers decide which of your floor plans they like best. This vital decision is part of the main road on your map toward the sale. While there may be many detours off this main road during the demonstration, you will always want to keep track of where the main road is, and how to get back to it before you drift too far away. Throughout the demonstration, help your customers maintain clear focus on the primary goal – choosing a favorite home. Customers who "love" all of your homes equally, or who keep trying to mix and match the best features, will need to move beyond that mindset if they are ever going to buy a home.

If customers drift off course with irrelevant questions, you may be able to use those questions to build rapport. But remember that your goal is *always simplify, never complicate*. If a customer repeatedly tries to steer you off the main road and thwart your efforts to get back, or if they are unwilling to make any of the decisions you present, they may not be "ready, willing and able" to buy a home yet. This is when you may want to step back and ask a question that will enable them to express larger concerns. An example of this kind of question would be, *"How are you feeling about the whole idea of buying a home at this point?"*

7. Create a sense of anticipation for the home sites you are about to show them.

We have said that one of the objectives of every stage of the sale is to lead into the next stage. Your goal is always to **get the customer to want to go farther.** In each stage of the sale, create excitement for the next stage as well as the current one. Once a customer chooses a favorite house type, you are then able to set up the next stage of the sale – the trip to the sites.

One obvious opportunity to create anticipation for your home sites is while you are standing at the site plan in the sales office. However, the model demonstration may provide you another opportunity. As you are walking through the model with customers, you could stop at a rear window and begin talking about your sites, using the model lot as a frame of reference.

If your sites are one of your advantages, then you want to create anticipation for them as early as possible. Even if they are only average, once the customer has picked out a particular style of home, the next goal is to get them to pick out a favorite home site.

You want to move them into this next stage as seamlessly as possible by saying, *"The next thing I'd like to do is show you where these homes are located. While we're looking at them, it will also give you a chance to get a better understanding of what the neighborhood is (will be) like."*

Showing Home Sites

For many top salespeople, showing home sites is the most exciting part of the selling process. Perhaps even more significant is the fact that visiting home sites is the most exciting part of the home buying process for many customers. Whether the home site has a completed home on it, or a home under construction, or whether it is a raw lot that is not even graded, the home site is where the *adventure* is. Your goal in showing home sites is to enrich the adventure, and to set up the close. Many salespeople even try to complete the close at the home site, where "one-of-a-kind" urgency has been created.

The home site is a wonderful "selling arena." You are away from the formal, merchandised environment of the sales office and models. You are outdoors. It is casual. You are away from distractions and interruptions. You have shown your customers they are worth your special attention, and they have told you they want that attention. Your selling momentum is full speed ahead.

While the purpose of the other selling arenas is to advance the sale, the purpose of this one is to complete the sale. Never let your focus waver from the close, even when the selling situation causes you to make detours. Detours are fine, as long as your focus on closing brings you back.

Here are some ways to maximize your effectiveness in the "home site arena."

1. If your home sites are one of the more important features, then you should place more emphasis on the site-showing stage of the selling process.

This is an obvious principle, but it is worth mentioning in order to make two points:

• If your home sites are a significant part of your value package, then your goal must be to get every viable prospect out to your sites. Sometimes this could even mean taking people to your sites before they have selected a favorite model.

• If your home sites are not very good, it means that you may have to take the selling process farther toward the close (including creating urgency) before you take customers to see your home sites. The customers' urgency may have to be based more upon their desire to improve their lives by living in your home and community than upon a "one-of-a-kind" urgency.

2. Create a sense of anticipation for the home sites before you reach the point of asking the customer to visit them.

If you have desirable home sites, begin building your transition to the site-showing stage by talking about the desirability of the sites during an earlier phase of the presentation, such as standing at the site plan display or walking through the models. *Anticipation increases impact,* so if customers are prepared for something exciting, they will be more likely to perceive it as exciting when they see it. The challenge here is to make sure you don't oversell in advance. While you want to create positive anticipation, you must still be sure the customer's expectations are met. The same principle applies with major objections, which is our next item.

Decide in advance what you like about each home site, or why you think someone else would choose it. Every home site has a buyer. Be able to say to a customer, "The reason I want you to see this site is…" The trip to the home sites is not just an expedition. Like every other stage of the sale, it needs a *sense of purpose.* You are not merely looking at home sites, you are finding the right one for them.

3. If you have a particular issue about any home sites that you know will create anxiety when you get there, bring up the issue in advance to test the water.

Some issues are only objections for certain people. If you don't know whether your particular customer will have that objection, you may choose to wait until you reach the site to get the customer's reaction. However, if you are reasonably sure the objection will arise, try to explain and defuse it *before* the customer sees it – remove the *yikes factor.* The magnitude of the objection increases when it takes the customer by surprise. Unpleasant surprises can quickly destroy momentum.

4. Remember that many customers will compromise their demands for a great home site if they are getting a great home, community and value otherwise.

If your home sites are not very special, don't be discouraged when customers initially demand a first-class site. The truth is that most people do not buy great home sites. They buy the best total value for the money, with home, location, community and price usually ranking higher than the lot. Some people really do demand a terrific home site because it is truly a top priority for them. You may lose those customers. But a far greater number of customers are willing to compromise on the home site in order to obtain their other priorities for a better price.

5. Sell the neighborhood.

For some buyers, your neighborhood may be even more important than your homes. While you have probably already made some reference to your neighborhood prior to the site-showing stage, this is the time to bring the community to life. Without invading privacy or violating the spirit of the EHO laws, tell enough about the community, the neighbors and the amenities to let your prospects know that it is a nice place to live – a community they would enjoy being a part of.

Anecdotes about other people who have bought your homes have an impact that other kinds of information do not have, because customers can relate to anecdotes on a more human level. The same principle relates to third-party endorsements that you can pass on from previous buyers.

6. Display your expertise.

Customers want to know they are buying from an expert. Use engineering plans, architectural blueprints and your own knowledge to show that you understand the specifics of the home site's engineering and the home's construction process. You are not using your expertise to bore the customer with tedious details, but rather to enhance the adventure of visiting the sites, and build customer confidence in you and your builder. Expertise is as valuable as rapport for increasing the customer's comfort level. Expertise also increases perceived value.

7. Walk on to the home site, not just up to it.

There is a huge difference between walking *to* the site and then pointing when you get there as opposed to actually walking around *on* the site. Walking on the site is the first tangible step toward ownership. It takes the adventure to the next level. Remember that when you are showing home sites, you are not just selling a home, you are creating a vision. "Emotional selling" is just as important in showing sites as it is in showing homes. Selling new homes is as much an art as it is a craft.

8. Get customers involved in the activity of the demonstration.

As you go to the home sites with engineering and architectural plans and the appropriate rulers (engineer's and architect's rulers have more impact than a twelve-inch ruler), take along a 100-foot tape as well. Standing on the lot, you will show the size and shape of the yards, how drainage will work, and where the home will be sited. As you measure off the important distances in areas where grading and construction have not been started (distance from the home to the street, to side and rear property lines, and to future homes), have the customer hold one end of the tape while you walk with the other end to your point of destination. Also use the tape to explain future grading by moving your end of the tape up to the height of the grade change once you have gone the appropriate distance. It is also impressive if you can train yourself to take a pace of exactly two feet or three feet for areas where the tape becomes too cumbersome or is not long enough.

Even if construction has not been started on the home, you can still "walk through the home" on the vacant home site by using the blueprints and the appropriate measurements. This is another way of creating involvement and bringing the home to life – important parts of the adventure of visiting the home site. This effort will help customers understand the views from each of the rooms, and the effects of sunlight during different times of the day.

9. Help customers enjoy the experience of seeing homes under construction.

If you are showing a site on which a home has already been started, consider that seeing a home under construction is one of the adventures that enriches the buying experience for customers. It is also an experience they will not always get, because many salespeople try to sidestep that part of the sale. Perhaps they don't feel comfortable with their construction knowledge. Sometimes they just don't enjoy going to homes under construction themselves. Or possibly they think the experience will be difficult for their customers. On the contrary, seeing a home under construction helps to create involvement if it is led effectively by a skilled salesperson.

If customers are unfamiliar with seeing a home under construction, you may need to create a sense of positive anticipation for the experience in advance. You can say, *"The home I want to show you is currently in the framing stage. Many people feel that's the best time to look at a home, because you can not only see how the home lays out, you can also see how it's built."* Now the customers have a sense of purpose about seeing a home in this stage. They feel they would be missing out on part of the home buying experience by not seeing a home under construction.

Salespeople who have developed skills for showing homes under construction usually have a very high closing ratio with those customers they get out on to the site. Therefore, the more customers they can get to the site, the more homes they will sell.

Construction knowledge should be one of the top priorities of a new home salesperson. Customers want to buy from experts. They will attach an intangible but very real value factor to homes that are sold by experts. Expertise builds credibility, and credibility builds value.

For many home buyers, gaining knowledge is one of the ways they get emotionally involved. Customer involvement is not just about "imagine yourself living here at Christmas." It is also about gaining a better understanding of what they are buying, how it will improve their quality of life, and why it is a better home for the money than anyone else's.

Every minute you spend learning construction will be a profitable investment of your time. You are selling a complex product. The fact that a customer is buying a new home instead of a resale may mean that today's superior building process is important to them, whether they say so or not. Sometimes they will ask construction questions, and sometimes they won't. When they don't, spend a little time explaining a few highlights about your construction that you have prepared in advance. If they tell you they are not interested, then you can move on, but this will be rare. Assume your customer is interested in whether your homes are well built, how your construction compares with the competition, and how your own expertise compares with that of other salespeople. You don't have to spend too much time on it, but a few minutes will give you one more advantage.

Even if you are explaining a feature that your competition also offers, the fact that you are the one explaining it puts you ahead.

The more a buyer can perceive you as a "builder," and not just a "salesperson," the more comfortable they will feel in their purchase.

One salesperson I worked with prepares his customers for the process by saying, *"I'll show you our models to give you an idea of what's included and how our homes feel. Then we can go down the street and I'll give you an idea of how we build them. We're well known for our construction standards."*

Some salespeople fear that the customer's level of excitement will drop when they go to a home under construction after they have seen decorated models. Yet the customer's excitement level can increase when a skilled salesperson is there to enrich the experience.

Customers realize the home is in the process of being built. They don't expect glamour. They want information, and they delight in adventure. After all, that's part of buying a new home. Customers get to see the construction process unfold.

It is important not to appear self-conscious about showing homes at various stages of incompletion. Customers need to see that you are comfortable selling homes this way. It will make them more comfortable knowing that people also buy homes this way.

Don't apologize or say, "I know it's going to be difficult to imagine what this home will look like when it's finished." You are the expert. If you say it's difficult to view a home under construction, then it's difficult. If you say it's easy, then it's easy. Take them through a home under construction much as you would a finished home. You may need to give a little more explanation of the rooms to help orient the customer, but otherwise sell the basic features and benefits as though you were in a model. Ask for feedback from customers periodically to make sure they visualize what you are showing them. Usually they will, but if they don't, then you know you must devote a little more time to explanation. For most customers, the experience of walking through a framed home grows on them as they progress, and it becomes easier for them to understand as they become more comfortable with it.

Explain as simply as possible what a room will look like when it is finished. Then ask, *"Are you picturing this okay?"* Also, ask customers what they think from time to time, to be sure they are relating to the home and progressing through the decision-making process. Tell why other people have liked particular features, and why you like them, too. This is another way to "bring the home to life."

For rooms that are especially hard to visualize, some salespeople draw furniture placements on the subfloor with chalk.

Don't worry that something may be wrong in the home under construction. Getting everything right in a home is a process that continues until the home is completed. You don't need to have everything right in order to show a home. You just need to be able to explain the process. For example, if there is water in the basement, explain the ways that water gets into a basement prior to final grading and installation of gutters and windows. Explain that the materials are water-resistant because water is expected. Explain why there should be no water once the home is completed, and how your warranty process works in case of something unforeseen.

Showing homes under construction is a valuable selling opportunity. Prepare your field presentation as you would your sales office and model presentations. Then get as many prospects as possible out on to the construction site in order to keep the sale moving toward the close.

10. Lead the customer to pick out a favorite home site.

Picking the favorite home site is one of the most important objectives for completing the selling process and moving toward the close. As with the other stages of the sale, your goal in showing home sites is not merely to allow customers to see your selection, but to get them to *make a decision* – to pick out a favorite.

Use many of the same feedback questions discussed for picking out a favorite home type.

Every home site is unique. When they pick out a favorite site, you can begin to create "one-of-a-kind" urgency through fear of loss. There is a very real possibility that the next customer who walks in the door will feel the same way your current customer does. This leaves the current customer with a choice of making a decision now, or possibly settling for their second choice later because someone else was more decisive.

Once they have made the decision, be sure they have articulated *why* they chose that home site.

Use your expertise not only to instill confidence, but also to help your customers make decisions. Don't just "show" your home sites. Be willing to *guide* your customers if you feel it would help them. You may occasionally have to go out on a limb by suggesting which of your sites you feel might be best for them. This is one way to create a sense of interest, or positive anticipation, for customers who visit your home sites. Your suggestion may be based on information they have already given you concerning their preferences. If they have not provided such information, you can take your best shot based on your own judgment, and let them agree or disagree. If they disagree and prefer a different home site, there is no harm done. You do not have to defend your position. You have still helped them to make a decision.

11. Set up the close.

As we said earlier, the home sites are where many top salespeople ask for the sale, because they believe this is the moment when the customer's emotions and sense of urgency reach their peak. Others prefer to proceed to the details of financing and then ask for the sale. In the latter case it can still be helpful to present the buying scenario once before the final closing moment comes, so when it does arrive it is more familiar. An example of this strategy would be to say, at some point during the home site visit, *"When folks decide to buy a home here, what we do is write up a purchase agreement which includes a deposit of $5000. The rest is due when you move in."* With this approach you not only prepare them for the close which is coming, you also get an opportunity to test their initial reaction to this information without requiring a commitment.

Closing The Sale

I once asked a top salesperson what made him so effective in his technique. He told me, "From the minute a customer walks in the door, I stay focused on getting them to make decisions. As long as they're making decisions, I'm making progress."

We have said that a success mentality in new home sales includes *a desire to resolve things*. Closing means getting customers to make *a series of decisions* that ultimately lead to the decision to buy. Throughout the selling process we try to discern buying signals. A customer's willingness to make *preliminary decisions* is the truest buying signal of all. If you can keep getting feedback from customers that says you are fulfilling their needs, and if you can keep giving customers opportunities to make preliminary decisions, then you are closing.

The idea of closing sometimes seems intimidating, especially to newer salespeople. Yet closing can be the easiest and most natural part of the sale. Closing is simply helping people make a decision, and leading them through the steps which lead to that decision. Once you have done this, it is only natural that you should ask them what their decision is. Sometimes the decision will not go your way. Still, if you can do a better job than anyone else of helping the customer through this decision-making process, it will go your way often enough.

We are told that before we can execute an effective close, we must **earn the right to close**. What this means is that we must successfully complete the stages that set up the close in order for the close to be natural.

What makes closing easy is the fact that once we have gone through the selling process, **the customer expects us to close**. Customers expect salespeople in any business to learn their needs, explain how the product fulfills their needs, and then ask them to buy it. From the customer's standpoint, that is professional salesmanship.

*   *   *

I asked another top closer the following question: "Suppose you had a situation in which you had gone through the entire selling process with a customer. They had picked a home, picked a lot, and you knew they were qualified. But you also knew that if you asked them to buy that day, they would say no. What would you do then?"

Without any hesitation he said, "I'd ask them to buy."

"Why would you do that if you knew the answer would be no?" I asked.

"I don't care if they say yes or no," he answered. "That's not why I ask them to buy. I ask them to buy in order to fulfill their expectation of me." Then he explained what he meant. "Put yourself in the buyer's shoes," he said. "They know I'm a salesperson. If I spend a couple of hours showing them what I have and telling them why they should buy it, and then I don't ask them to buy it, they'll wonder what's going on." Then he concluded, "I think of closing as an invitation to be a member of my community." This salesperson had no fear of rejection. To him, rejection was not even an issue. His only fear was that he would make his customers feel unwanted if he did not ask them to buy.

*   *   *

We want to set up the close by creating a situation in which the close is the next natural step to take – where the customer would be surprised if we don't ask for the sale. The more decisions we get from our customers along the way, the more natural the close becomes.

In one sense, everything we have discussed in this book up to now has been about closing, so now it is time to look back on each stage of the sale to see how it actually does relate to closing.

Closing involves a **closing process** – the series of smaller decisions that lead to the final decision to buy – and **a closing moment** – the moment when we offer our customers the opportunity to turn their decisions into action. Before we get to the closing moment, let's first review how the entire selling process leads the customer to that final closing moment. Then I will discuss a variety of ways the final closing moment can occur. We will explore ideas for how to set up the close in order to make it easier and more natural; how to complete the close; and how to proceed when our attempts to close are unsuccessful.

THE CLOSING PROCESS

The more effective you are at the closing process, the more natural the closing moment will be. Selling, in its most ideal form, is **raising the customer's comfort level to the point where the close becomes inevitable.** The goal of the closing process is to make the closing moment easy.

The closing process begins with the customer's first decision. Sometimes the early decisions seem to come easily. The customer opens up to you right away, describing his or her situation, level of motivation, top priorities, and ability to buy. One decision flows easily into the next because the customer is already focused on his mission.

More often, however, your customers' decisions result from the questions you ask. Your questions provide the framework for the closing process. In the early stages of your relationship with the customer, look for comfortable opportunities to ask the kinds of questions that can get the decision process started. As your customers consider these questions, you are beginning to create a *decision-making rhythm* in the interaction.

Some customers are not very interactive in the beginning, yet they are still willing to listen if they are interested in what you are saying. In this case, just go on about the business of presenting your initial overview. Even the overview relates to the closing process: it helps you set the stage in the customer's mind about what makes your homes and community special.

The closing process includes five primary benchmarks by which to measure your progress:

1. Identify the customer's needs.
2. Convey your basic selling message (or concept).
3. Lead the customer to select a favorite home.
4. Lead the customer to select a favorite home site.
5. Ask for the sale.

THE CLOSING MOMENT

The closing process leads ultimately to the closing moment when you ask for the sale.

Occasionally the final decision to buy will not be made in your presence. In some cases, you may not even see it coming. Your interaction with some customers may end with them telling you nothing more than, "Thank you for your time." Then they leave, seeming lukewarm at best. Yet several days later they return to your sales office and say, "We're ready to buy." It may be someone with whom you had not even planned to follow up. Their decision to buy takes you completely by surprise. Most of us have experienced this situation at least once. We feel reluctant to take any credit at all for closing the sale. While this kind of sale may occur from time to time, it is not the kind through which you will make a living.

In most of your sales, there is a real closing process that leads to a specific closing moment. Sometimes customers will close themselves. They may say something like, "We really like this. If we decide to buy it, what's the next step?" Other times you may need to take a modest initiative, yet the close still seems very easy. But most of the time you will clearly be the one who makes the closing moment happen.

Your goal with the closing process is always to make the closing moment as easy and natural as possible. This is part of what we mean by the phrase "earning the right to close." Often the success of your closing efforts results not so much from how the close itself is executed, but from how well you execute the stage right before the close – how well you "set up the close."

The kinds of feedback questions and decision questions you have been using along the way help pave the way for the close. Although some customers make the decision to purchase by themselves, most often customers are progressing through the process, yet still need help in turning their thoughts into decisions, and their decisions into action. You know they are not quite ready to make a final decision, but you also believe that, with a little help, they can get there. You need a way to help them pull all of their thoughts and feelings together in order to create a focus for what they plan to do. To put it another way, you want to help them *build a transition to the close.* These are the moments for which you need a strategy for setting up the close.

SETTING UP THE CLOSE

We have said that questions create the framework for the closing process. We discussed the kinds of questions that create a decision-making rhythm as the customer is experiencing your homes and home sites. Now you are ready to take your questions to the next level. The feedback questions evolve into questions that help your customers clarify their own feelings, and turn these feelings into action. These are the questions that set up the close, making the final closing moment easier, more natural, and more successful. Examples of questions that set up the close are as follows:

- *"Do you feel as though you're making some progress?"*
- *"Is this what you were looking for?"* *("...hoping for?")*
- *"From what you've seen so far, what do you think?"*
- *"When you first came in, you mentioned that you were looking for _____. How does this compare to what you were hoping for?"*
- *"From what you told me earlier, it looks like we've found what you were looking (hoping) for."* [Just make this statement and then wait for the customer to respond.]
- *"Is all this looking pretty good to you?"*
- *"Do you have a good feeling about all this?"* *("I have a really good feeling about this. How about you?")*
- *"I get the feeling you really like (want) this home. Is that true?"*
- *"How do you feel about the idea of living here?"* *("Do you think you'd enjoy living here?")* *("Can you see yourself living here some day?")*
- *"Are we a possibility for you?"*
- *"Do you think we might get the chance to have you as a customer (neighbor)?"*
- *"Do you think we might fit into your future plans?"*
- *"What is your game plan at this point?"*

*   *   *

Sometimes we find ourselves moving into the closing stages of the sale without really knowing where we stand. Despite our best efforts to get feedback from our customers as we go, we still do not have a good feeling about whether or not we will be able to close the sale that day. We want to move toward the close, but we do not want to rush it. We want to bring the interaction to a positive conclusion without making the customer feel pushed. We want to close gradually and gently, giving the customer time to warm up to the fact that we are closing, and to organize their thoughts in the most favorable way possible.

In situations like this I think back to childhood when we would play the game of trying to find a treasure that someone has hidden from us. We walk into the room where the item is hidden and begin to look around. If there is someone else in the room who knows where the treasure is, we ask, "Am I getting warm?" As we get closer we ask, "Am I getting hot?" Finally we ask, "Is it here?"

Perhaps this childhood game could relate to closing. Use your questions in a 3-stage close to clarify with your customer if you are getting warm, hot, or if they would like to buy. This would allow you to approach the close more gradually when you feel you need to, but still approach it with a sense of purpose.

A 3-stage close could occur as you are standing on the home site the customer has selected as their favorite, or as you are walking back to the sales office from the site. It could also take place at your desk after you have finished reviewing the numbers. First you want to find out where you stand. Then you want to move into the actual closing question. The 3-stage close could work like this:

1. Am I warm?

- *"How is all this looking to you?"*
- *"How does all this feel to you?"*
- *"Does this look like it's coming together for you?"*
- *"What do you think? Are the pieces fitting together?"*

There are many possible variations on the wording of this question, depending upon the customer and the exact situation of the moment. The point is to have an initial question which tests the water to see if there is immediate resistance to the idea of making a buying decision. If the customer derails you with a negative answer to this question, then you can deal with the issue before attempting a true close. If you get a response that is enthusiastically favorable, you could skip your second question and go directly to the close. This would be like asking, "Am I getting warm?" and being told, "Yes. In fact, you're getting hot." However, if you get a mildly favorable response ("Yes, you're getting warm"), then you can move on to your next "pre-close" question.

2. Am I hot?
- *"Is this what you're looking for?"*
- *"Do you feel like there are any loose ends?"*
- *"Dos this look like something you'd be happy with?"*
- *"Does this look like the one?"*
- *"Have you found what you were hoping for?"*

The customer's response to this question might propel you to a confident close, such as, *"Let's go back and write it up."* On the other hand, the response may seem favorable but ambivalent, leading you to ask your final question more cautiously. If their responses to the first two questions have kept the sale moving forward, but you still feel you need to close more delicately, then you would go to the third stage.

3. Would you like to buy?
You can explain the buying process (contract, loan application, walkthrough, settlement) and then offer the customer the buying opportunity.
- *"When folks decide they'd like to live here, what they do is..."* [Explain the process]... *"Are you at that point?"* (*"Would you like to do that?"*)
- *"When folks decide this is what they want, we take the home off the market with..."* [Explain process]... *"Would you like me to take this home off the market for you?"*

If you would prefer to ask a closing question rather than explain the process, here are three examples of wording for a cautious close:

- *"Do you feel ready to go to the next stage (to take the next step)?"*
- *"Do you feel you want to discuss it a little further, or would you like to move forward?"*
- *"Are there any issues you need to resolve in order to make a decision you'll feel good about?"*

There is nothing better than a confident close. You want to take a confident approach whenever you can. However, in those occasional situations where you feel that a confident close will not work, the 3-stage close suggested here is better than no close at all.

Many times a smooth transition from the closing process to the closing moment will be the most important stage of the sale – the stage that could determine whether or not your attempts to close will be successful.

COMPLETING THE CLOSE

One of the hardest things about closing for many salespeople is the fear that the attempt to close will fail, and the sale will be "blown." This causes some salespeople to back off from the final close. How do you know when you've reached the final closing moment? How do you know whether to go for it?

When the customers have picked out a favorite home and a favorite home site, and you have given them the information they need in order to make a decision, and you have determined that they are able buyers, then you have reached the point where you have "earned the right to close." If they give you a tangible buying signal at that point, then everything is perfect. "Strike while the iron is hot," whether it is their first visit or their fifth. Simple enough.

The tough part comes when a customer has picked out a favorite home and home site, but then does not give a tangible buying signal. How do you know whether or not to close at that point? What if you try to close and fail?

If you have accomplished all of the necessary stages that lead up to the close, and therefore have earned the right to close, then, with rare exceptions, you should always close.

Can any harm result if they reject your attempt to close them? Would you have been better off if you had not tried, even though you successfully got through all the stages leading up to the close? It is very unlikely that you would lose a sale because you asked for it. In fact, it may be the actual closing question that creates the first urgency to buy. This can happen when the closing question causes buyers to **confront themselves** in their own minds with the question, "Now that I have the opportunity to improve my life, what will it mean if I say no? Am I really serious about improving my life, or is this just a hopeless fantasy?" They may surprise you by deciding they want to go ahead with it once they have worked through this internal confrontation, or they may need to wrestle with it a little more at home. But at least you have brought the decision to the forefront of their consciousness, where it belongs.

At this stage in the selling process, the issue is not whether the close succeeds or fails. By always closing when you reach the closing moment, you will at least know that you took the sale as far as you could that day. You won't be left watching a customer walk out and not knowing what would have happened if you had tried to close.

When you don't see any buying signals, consider whether any of these possibilities could apply to your customer.

- Some buyers are simply not motivated to give buying signals.
- Some may not be very expressive by nature, especially in situations where they feel vulnerable.
- Some may not feel comfortable giving buying signals. They may feel that they need to be actively "sold" rather than take

the buying initiative themselves.

- They may be giving buying signals that you are not aware of.
- They may have given the most important buying signal of all – a willingness to make the preliminary decisions – without showing the enthusiasm you were hoping for.

*   *   *

A customer's answer to one of your setup questions could make your close obvious, or perhaps even unnecessary. That would be ideal.

Sometimes, however, the close is not so easy, yet it is still necessary. Many customers will simply not close themselves, no matter how well you prepare them or set up the close. They need help in the form of a direct closing question in order to take the action that will improve their lives.

One approach, as in the "3-stage close," is to explain the buying process and then ask the customer to respond. For example, you could say, *"When folks decide they want to take a home off the market here, the way it works is..."* Then you explain the process for buying a home. After that, you could ask a question such as, *"What do you think?"* or, *"Are you ready to do that?"* or, *"Would you like to take this home off the market?"*

You know this moment is coming, so you are prepared and relaxed. If you appear confident in your closing approach, it will help increase the customer's own comfort level with the moment.

There will be other times when you do not feel you need to explain the process. You just want to go ahead and get the question out on the table. Again, you want to be sure you have a question with which you are comfortable.

- *"Would you like to go ahead and take this home off the market?"* (*"Would you like me to go ahead and take this home off the market for you?"*)
- *"Would you like to have this home?"*

- *"Is this the one for you?"* (*"Have you found the one for you?"*) (*"Have you found the home that will make you happy?"*) (*"Have you found what you were looking for?"*)
- *"Are you ready to go ahead with the next step?"*
- *"Would you like to see how this looks on paper?"* (*"Would you like to start going over some of the forms?"*) (*"Would you like to go ahead and start the paperwork?"*)
- *"If you are interested in going ahead with the next step, what we would do is..."* [Explain the next step.] *"Would you like to do that?"*

Sometimes salespeople are worried about being too aggressive with their close. You certainly do not want to rush the close, but you do not want to appear reluctant either. As long as your close is respectful, and has been "earned," you normally do not need to worry about being too aggressive. ***Think of closing as a compliment.***

Even if you are accidentally too aggressive with your close, most customers will forgive you once. They know you are a salesperson, and a close that is too aggressive can be forgiven one time as enthusiasm. The second time you close the same customer too aggressively, it could run the risk of becoming disrespectful.

* * *

There may be times when you feel you should be zeroing in on the final close, yet you feel that something is wrong, and you can't put your finger on it. In this case your closing efforts may include questions designed to uncover concerns or negative feelings that the customer is not expressing. You need to know the customer's true feelings and intentions. Some people feel that asking customers to express negative feelings is too risky. On the other hand, if customers have concerns, it is better for them to wrestle with their concerns in your presence than in your absence. Examples of these kinds of questions include:

- *"Is there anything about this home you don't like?"* (*"...that doesn't work for you?"*) (*"...that concerns you?)* (*"...that you don't feel good about?"*)
- [If the customer does raise a concern, and you want to find out whether their concern will really make a difference in their decision]: *"Other than that, how do you feel about the home?"*
- *"Are there any issues you need to resolve in order to make a decision you'll feel good about?"*
- *"Is all this working out like you were hoping it would?"*
- *"On a scale of one to ten, how do you like what you've seen here?...What is it that's between us and a ten?"*

*   *   *

It is important for new salespeople not to view closing as intimidating. It is a perfectly natural conclusion to everything that has gone before. Don't worry if your close "fails." Even when your close is "rejected" ("no" is not really a rejection, it is only an answer), it brings the customer's decision-making mechanism into play and keeps it there. Customers know you are a salesperson who asks for the sale. They are now preconditioned that the next time they visit, you will ask them again. They will have to prepare their thoughts accordingly.

Sometimes when customers keep coming back without buying, it is because we never asked them. We have "trained" them that we won't require any decision of them. They respond by coming back again and again with "a few more questions," and no intention of buying.

Closing – creating a decision-making process and then bringing it to a conclusion (whether the customer buys that day or not) – not only enables you to maximize your opportunity that day, but may also increase your chances of selling a home to that customer in the near future.

IS THERE LIFE AFTER A CLOSE THAT FAILS?

We have been discussing three elements of confident, successful closing:

- A closing process that focuses on a series of decisions.
- A strategy for setting up the close to make it as easy and natural as possible.
- A comfortable way to ask for the sale when the closing moment finally arrives.

There is still one more piece you need in order to complete the closing puzzle. Just as you need to be prepared in advance with your game plans for the closing process, setting up the close, and completing the close, you also need to be prepared with a plan for what you will do when you ask customers to buy and they say no. At this point you want to find out where you stand, and what the customers' future intentions regarding your home may be. Is there any chance they may buy your home? If there is, what hurdles must be overcome?

Here are a few suggestions for keeping your interaction moving in a positive direction when your attempt to close does not result in an immediate sale.

In some situations the natural response is simply to ask customers point-blank why they are not buying. For example, you could say, *"I know there are a lot of things about this home you really like."* You can review the things they liked about the home, and then ask, *"Is there anything you don't like?"* (*"Are there any concerns we didn't address?"*)

You also want to be sure they remain comfortable in the relationship after "rejecting" your attempt to close. They need to feel wanted, not pressured. Tell them, *"I've really enjoyed getting to spend this time with you, and I hope we're able to have you as a customer (neighbor) at some point."* Then you could continue by asking, *"Are there any other concerns I can help you with?"* (*"Is there anything about this home that you're still not quite comfortable with?")*

You may want to ask them where they are in their buying decision. *"I know you're not ready to make a final decision today. What is your game plan at this point? (What will be your next step?)"*

If they respond that they want to look at a few more communities, you can still try to get them to resolve their feelings about your homes. You could ask, *"If you don't see anything else you like as well as what you've seen here, do you think this is a home you'd be happy with?"*

Or you could simply ask, *"Will I be seeing you again soon?"* In cases like this you are merely testing the water to see if your customers have anything else on their mind that you need to know about in order to keep the sale moving.

Perhaps you have the opportunity to ask your customers what it is that will close them. For example, the customer may say, "I'm not going to buy anywhere until I know I'm getting the best deal." You could then ask, *"How will you know when you're getting the best deal?"* Another example of this approach could be: *"I know you're concerned about making the right decision, but how will you know when you've found the right home?"* Always be on the lookout for opportunities where customers can tell you how to sell them a home.

When customers have expressed dissatisfaction with their current home, you may have an opportunity to reinforce the fact that buying your home is the decision that will lead them to a better life. For example: *"We talked about how great it will be when you finally do get a new home, and it seems from what you have said that life really will be a lot better for you here (…that you'll be very happy here)."* Then just wait for them to respond. You could also say, *"By November, when this home is completed, would you rather be living here, or in the place where you live now?"*

Another approach could be to ask them how close they are to buying. An example of this type of question would be: *"On a scale of one to ten, with ten meaning you'd buy the home, how much do you like it?"* If they answer five or higher, then you could ask, *"What is it that's standing between you and a ten?"*

What about the customer who keeps coming back, but can't seem to make a decision? You feel as though you need a way to give them a push, and yet you don't want to demean them. Here we are getting into a more sensitive area. You feel that you need to take some special action in order to resolve the sale, one way or the other. You want to find out if they are merely a "pretender," and yet you don't want to push someone away who could have been a real buyer.

You may want to see if they can articulate their ambivalence. You could ask:

- *"How do you feel about the idea of living here?"*
- *"Do you think you'd be happy here (...happy with this home)?"*
- *"Is there anything you don't think you'd be happy with?"* (*"Is there anything about this that doesn't work for you?"*) (*"Is there anything about this that doesn't seem right?"*)

You also might consider advising them in order to help break their mental logjam.

- *"Would you like to know what I would do?"*
- *"Here's what I would do if I were in your shoes..."*
- *"From everything you've told me, what I would suggest is..."*

Here are a few other approaches for customers who are "on the fence."

- *"I get the feeling you really do like this home. Is that true?"...* [Wait for answer]...*"Is there anything about it that doesn't work for you?"...* [Wait for answer]... *"Most people who get as far as you have gotten and come back for a third time wind up living here. Is there anything in particular that's holding you back?"*
- *"Let me just ask you the obvious question. Do you think you'd*

be happy here?...Is there anything you don't think you'd be happy with?...You seem like you want to go ahead and get this over with so you can get on with your life."

- *"If this is the home for you, I want to be sure you're the one who gets it. If you feel good about this home, but just need a little more time to be sure, we can work out a way to take it off the market for you. Would that help?"* [Since this approach may involve a short-term lot hold to help the buyer take a small step when they are afraid to take a larger one, it is a judgment call. Many salespeople and managers are opposed to lot holds altogether.]

Some salespeople attempt to create fear of loss by asking customers to pick a second choice: *"I can certainly understand not wanting to move too fast. You don't want to make a decision you'll regret. While you're here, as long as you've picked out your favorite, which one is your second choice?"*

The customer might wonder why you asked such a question. You can explain, *"The reasons you picked that home site make good sense. Usually when we have one site that is better than the others, there is a pretty good chance it will be the next one to sell. We sell an average of one home a week here, so your first choice may only stay unsold for another week or two."*

This is a gentle way of getting them to face the consequences of failing to act. Naturally, you would not use this approach with anyone who is not close to buying. But it could create the necessary urgency for the customer who really wants what you are selling, but doesn't see any reason to act quickly.

Once you have maximized your opportunities for that day, then comes the time to set up your follow up call: *"I really appreciate you spending this time with me, and I've enjoyed talking with you. Do you mind if I keep in touch with you to see how your search is coming?"*

When you are prepared for the moment after the close, it can sometimes turn out to be the best selling opportunity of all.

CREATING URGENCY

One concept that is frequently associated with closing is "creating urgency." Just as the close cannot be created out of thin air in a single moment, neither can urgency.

We often become discouraged when customers come into our sales office with no apparent urgency to buy. We ask them, *"How soon are you planning to move?"* and they answer with something like, "We're in no hurry," or, "We're just looking." We think to ourselves, "Another looker. When will I get a decent prospect to work with?"

When we ask initial qualifying questions to determine a customer's level of motivation, we need to remember that many customers do not decide when they are going to move until after they have found the home they want. We must not reverse the chicken and egg here. Some customers, such as transferees, need to move right away. We know they will probably buy a home within the next two weeks, and we want them to buy ours. But what about the customers who don't need to move quickly? For top salespeople, these customers provide the overwhelming majority of their sales. Customers visit their sales offices with no immediate desire or need to buy, but then decide to buy because they want the home. This is a key element in successful selling.

We often think of creating urgency in terms of providing some kind of financial incentive. But top salespeople create urgency by getting customers to love their homes and believe they are the best, and by getting them to realize that as soon as they make the decision to buy, their quality of life will improve.

Urgency is created throughout the selling process, not just at the beginning or the end. Most customers cannot truly experience urgency until *after* they have decided they want your home. If you start hitting a customer too hard too early with messages such as, "You'd better act now, because they're going fast," or, "Let me tell you about our incentives," you will be using up all your ammunition before the customer is in range. It is okay to convey such information as a way of demonstrating activity. It may even have a positive impact by showing customers that exciting things are going on at your community. Just don't expect this kind of information to create urgency to buy until the customer has something to feel urgency about.

Circumstantial Urgency

It is true that sometimes customers will walk in your door with urgency to make a decision, such as the relocation buyer. Another example would be the customer whose lease is about to expire. Their urgency is being created partly by their circumstances. If they have already heard good things about your homes, their pre-conditioned sense of urgency may be even greater. *Circumstantial urgency* can be a very powerful force. When we think about urgency in new home sales, we are often thinking about circumstantial urgency. Sometimes the circumstances already exist on the buyer's end. Other times they can be created on the seller's side. Additional examples of circumstantial urgency on the buyer's end could include:

- The buyer's current home has just sold.
- They have to move soon for tax reasons.
- A baby is on the way and they need more room.
- Something has happened that has made their current living situation impractical or intolerable.

Ways that a seller can create circumstantial urgency include:

- The community is about to have a price increase.
- There is one home remaining that meets the customer's needs better than any of the others.
- The seller has a limited-time incentive program or special financing.

Our ability to create or take advantage of circumstantial urgency will increase our sales. However, with many customers we will not have those opportunities. We will have to create urgency from ground zero, with no circumstances on the part of the buyer or strategies on the part of the seller to help us. In these situations we need to look at urgency from a different perspective. We need to create urgency on the emotional level.

Emotional Urgency

How is *emotional urgency* created? Emotional urgency grows as the selling process progresses. If we try to create urgency too quickly at the beginning, we run the risk of being perceived as pushy or lazy. If we try to contrive sudden urgency at the end of the sale in an effort to close, we may be perceived as desperate. Creating urgency must never appear sudden or impatient, either at the beginning of the sale or at the end. Urgency must grow naturally, one step at a time, as you proceed through the various stages and decisions of the selling process.

This is how urgency works when people buy a car. They walk in saying, "We're just looking." Their old car still runs fine. There are plenty of cars on the lot, and other dealers within striking distance have their own selection and "special deals" for the same car. How does anyone in car sales ever create urgency? One step at a time.

The customer gets into the car and the salesperson explains a few features. As the customer gets more comfortable in the new car, the salesperson begins to ask questions about the old car. There must be something about the old car that the customer is dissatisfied with, or they wouldn't be out looking.

Often the urgency to buy a new car does not begin until the test drive. (This is like the model demonstration and the trip to the site in new home sales.) The test drive is where the customer becomes emotionally involved with the new car as the experience of enjoying it comes to life. The salesperson can now tap into the customer's desire to improve his life. She can ask, "How does this compare with your current car?" Before long she can begin to set up the close by asking, "Which car would you like to drive home in, this one or your old one?"

The process for selling new homes is similar. There are seven basic elements that create emotional urgency in new home sales.

1. The customers are unsatisfied with their current home.

Learn what it is about their current home that is unsatisfactory, and what their top priorities are for their next home. The more they can verbalize this information, the more you can use it to show how your home will meet their needs and improve their lives.

2. They must want your home.

Activate the emotional force in the buying decision by helping customers love your home. Ways to do this include:

- Showing how the home is what they are looking for (see #1 above).
- Telling why others have loved your homes, using anecdotes whenever they are helpful.
- Telling why you love your homes. Although you are the salesperson and are supposed to love your homes, you are also the expert. If you can explain why you love your homes, your enthusiasm will have genuine impact on your customers.
- Getting customers to talk about any positive feelings they have about your homes. Their ability to verbalize is as important as yours.
- Creating involvement through your demonstration, the information you give, and the questions you ask.

3. They must believe your home is the best available in your market.

While the emotional element in the buyer's decision-making process is important, the rational element must be there, too. Although emotions often get a head start on reason in many of life's major decisions, the rational part must catch up in order for the decision to be completed and acted upon. Customers must not only love your home, they must also believe it is the best. Showing why your home is best includes:

- Selling features and benefits.
- Showing the ways in which your homes are the best value (what your homes offer that others do not).
- Explaining what you set out to accomplish with your homes and community, and why other people have chosen your homes.
- Telling why you have chosen to sell them.
- Sharing why you have chosen to work for your company.

4. They must pick one home site from those you have available.

If you can successfully accomplish the first three items, then you are in a position to narrow down the customer's decision to "one of a kind." Help customers to choose a favorite site as well as a favorite home, and get them to articulate why they like that one best. If they can organize their thoughts into words, and then hear themselves say those words, it strengthens their conviction that they are on the right track.

5. They must realize that their favorite could be someone else's favorite, too.

"Fear of loss" begins here. Get them to understand that if one home and site is their favorite, it is likely to be other people's favorite as well. You could say, *"Your reasons for liking this home make a lot of sense. We've been getting very good response to it."*

6. They must believe they are in the right place at the right time.

Many people have strong feelings about the importance of timing in decisions. Look for opportunities to say, *"Your timing here is excellent."* Examples of timing benefits include:

- The construction schedule works with their planned moving time.
- They are just in time to get the options they want.
- The home next door just sold to some terrific neighbors.
- They are just in time to get your current price or incentive.

7. They must believe that the sooner they act, the sooner their lives will improve.

As we discussed earlier, there are some customers for whom urgency does not begin until you ask for the sale. For these buyers, it is actually the closing question itself that creates the urgency by causing them to confront the reality of their own intentions. This internal confrontation can sometimes be the most powerful motivator of all. The buyers must now say to themselves, "I set out to improve my life. Now I have the opportunity to do it. Why would I not improve my life today? What does it say about me if I say no?"

Creating urgency requires a balance of patience and impatience: the patience to allow customers to work through their issues, and the impatience to keep the process moving forward. The farther your customers get in the decision process, and the more involved they become in a particular home, the more successful you will be at creating emotional urgency, and capitalizing on circumstantial urgency.

Follow Up

I once had the opportunity to work with a successful veteran who, throughout his career, had maintained a diligent commitment to follow up. He sent letters, flyers and postcards, and was very consistent in his follow up by phone. Because this commitment had survived the test of time, I hoped to get some statistical tidbit from him about the success of his follow up efforts that I could use to encourage other salespeople. I asked him, "How many extra sales do you get each year because of your follow up?"

His answer surprised me. "I have no idea," he said.

I decided to persevere, assuming that he must have some way of tracking his success or he wouldn't have kept doing it. So I asked it another way. "How much extra money do you think you earn from your follow up efforts?"

I expected him to say something like $30,000 a year or $70 an hour. But again he said, "I really don't have any idea. I've never tracked it."

Then I asked, "What has made you stick with it all these years?"

He answered, "It's just the way I do business."

The more I thought about that answer, the more I realized what a perfect answer it was. He viewed follow up simply as one part of his overall superior approach to service.

Naturally, we want our follow up efforts to generate sales. Sometimes they will and sometimes they won't, so it is important not to think of follow up as a failure when it does not generate a sale. With a respectful, professional follow up call, the worst-case scenario is that you leave a customer feeling that you really want to sell them a home. How bad is that? If they feel that you value them and want to sell them a home more than any of your competitors, you have created one more competitive advantage. Research has shown that serious buyers appreciate follow up in any form, including calls, as long as it is respectful. They view it as a symbol of the professionalism and diligence they are seeking in a builder.

For many years, the primary follow up tool was the telephone. In the last few years, our telephone efforts have been impacted by three factors:

1. In many areas, telemarketing has become an increasing source of aggravation.

2. Caller ID, answering machines and voice mail have enabled people to screen their calls.

3. E-mail has become a more widely accepted form of communication.

In adjusting to these changes, we still need to think of follow up as a service that serious buyers value. Follow up is not an intrusion upon the prospect's privacy, but is the continuation of a relationship. If a follow up call reveals that a prospect has no intention of buying, or does not want us to call them any more, they will tell us, and we can move on. But if they are interested in buying a home from us, they will appreciate our care and diligence, as long as it is done with professionalism and respect.

You can begin to establish a positive tone for your follow up efforts before the customer leaves your sales office. If you can set the stage for your call while you are face to face with the customer, you will set yourself apart from telemarketers. Telemarketing often involves making a call that people don't want to receive in order to sell them something they don't want to buy. In new home sales, customers visit your community to determine whether they might be interested in buying one of your homes. You are also trying to determine whether one of your homes may be right for them. If they show an interest in what you are offering, then a follow up call becomes a service instead of an intrusion. You want to create a situation in which your follow up call is something they want, or at least will appreciate as part of your high level of service. The message you are conveying with your follow up efforts is, "I want to stay in touch because I value you as a customer."

One way to set up your follow up call is to tell them you will call them with a piece of information. When this is not possible, it is okay to tell them you want to call them simply to follow up with them. You could say, *"I really enjoyed getting the chance to meet with you, and I hope we're able to have you as a customer. I'd like to stay in touch. Would it be okay if I give you a follow up call?"* Or you could put your request in the form of a statement: *"I'll give you a call during the week to see if there's anything else I can do for you."* Now, if you do not have any other reason to follow up, you are calling to fulfill the expectation you set during the visit. The customer knows you are making a follow up call, and they know that follow up calls are an example of diligence and excellence, as long as they are done well.

Here are a few other ideas for creating an effective follow up program.

1. Give your follow up calls a sense of purpose.

A follow up call should say more than merely, "I just wanted to call to see if you had any questions." As in any part of selling, preparation is an important part of follow up. Preparation begins with the notes you write on the back of your guest card as soon as a customer leaves. Personalized information about your customers, highlights of their visit, product preferences, unresolved objections, and your game plan for follow up should be included.

In addition to being respectful and professional, you want your follow up call to be personal, warm and enthusiastic. Even your voice tone is important. A monotone implies indifference, which is the opposite of what you want your follow up call to convey. Preparation will help your tone as well as your content.

After introducing yourself and thanking the customer once again for visiting your community, you can convey whatever information you had planned. If you have no new information to give them, there is nothing wrong with simply saying, *"Now that you've had a few days to reflect back on your visit, do you think we may be a possibility for you?"*

One of the most important goals of a follow up call is to get an update on the customer's intentions. If they say they have some more places they want to see, you could still ask, *"If you don't see anything else you like as well as this, would you be happy here?"*

If you get any kind of hopeful response, then you could try for an appointment. *"I'd love to get a chance to talk with you some more. Could we set up a time to get together again?"*

2. Leave a message on an answering machine.

If you try to call several times and always get an answering machine, go ahead and leave a message. You might even prepare one in advance, so if you do get a machine, your message will come out smoothly. You still want the customer to know you care enough about them to follow up.

3. Consider e-mail.

E-mail has become more widely accepted as a follow up tool. Many guest cards now include a space for the customer's e-mail address. Some salespeople prefer the less invasive style that e-mail follow up offers, while others still prefer the more personal approach of phone calls and handwritten notes. The latter group may still use e-mail to set up their phone calls. Some customers are more comfortable responding to a salesperson by e-mail than by phone.

Of course, e-mail enables you to send information to many customers simultaneously, so you can contact more customers more quickly and frequently than ever before. A combination of personal e-mails to the best prospects plus generic ones to the rest can help you manage a larger prospect pipeline more efficiently.

4. Notes, letters and flyers are still effective.

Even in the age of e-mail, the personal note is still a valuable follow up tool. A handwritten, individualized note has the charm of special effort that e-mail was designed to eliminate.

At a busy community it may not be realistic to write a truly personal, meaningful note to everyone who visits you. Computer-generated letters to secondary prospects can be effective, as long as the customer's name is personalized and the letter is hand-signed. A handwritten P.S. can also enhance the impact of these more generic letters. Among the advantages of computer-generated letters are that they can be longer and can be sent more often, as long as the content is varied.

Flyers are less personal, but still offer the benefits of conveying information and showing longer-term prospects that you haven't forgotten about them.

5. Have a system for tracking prospects.

There are several popular ways to categorize prospects. One way is by the "A, B, C" system. Prospect cards are filed according to the salesperson's estimate of the prospect's likelihood of buying, with "A" prospects getting the highest level of attention, "B's" being contacted less frequently, and "C's" only occasionally.

Another way is by date. The salesperson's prospect file is organized by dates on which a follow up effort will be accomplished. The prospect file works like a calendar, and is sometimes called a "tickler file."

A third method is to combine the first two. With this system, separate tickler files are set up for the A, B and C prospects. The system triggers follow up actions by date, but also prioritizes them by likelihood of purchasing.

*   *   *

Many salespeople who are successful with follow up say that the most important key to their success is consistency. This does not necessarily mean contacting the same customer again and again. That is a case-by-case judgment call that depends upon the outcome of each contact. What they mean by consistency is simply sticking with it, even during those periods when results are discouraging. Since there is a hit-or-miss aspect to follow up, sometimes there will be more misses than others. Fortunately, the opposite also occurs. There will be times when your follow up efforts yield surprisingly high results for no apparent reason. The hot streak simply needs the chance to begin.

A consistent follow up program not only increases sales by enabling you to contact more customers more frequently and effectively, but the feedback you get from follow up (especially phone calls) also increases your overall awareness and control of your selling efforts. This produces the valuable fringe benefit of a higher level of confidence in your face-to-face interactions with your customers.

Managing Customers

One of the most important responsibilities of a new home salesperson is customer management. Salespeople with a success mentality try to establish a relationship with each buyer that is mutually gratifying. These salespeople seek to make every sale a source of satisfaction for themselves and their company. However, the satisfaction of their customers is also a top priority. To achieve mutual satisfaction, they focus on setting the correct expectations for every buyer. Then they do everything they can to make sure each expectation they set is met or exceeded. They provide the best possible service, yet still maintain control of their relationships with their buyers.

SETTING EXPECTATIONS

Customer management begins with setting expectations. The expectations our customers have of us will play a critical role in the satisfaction we provide them.

We sometimes assume that if we give customers everything they want, they will be satisfied. Yet we often feel thwarted in these efforts. A customer may seem happy one day and unhappy the next, satisfied at one point and then dissatisfied a little later. We cannot figure out what caused their feelings to change. We thought we were doing everything they wanted. We even bent over backwards to please them, giving them things to which they were not entitled by the original agreement, and they are still not happy. We try to go the extra mile to give our customers the best service possible. This is a fine attitude and a worthy mission. Why does it sometimes feel as though it isn't working? Because happiness and satisfaction are moving targets. Sometimes they move too fast for us to keep up with them. Even a customer's expectations of us can change. So where does all this leave us in our quest to set correct expectations and achieve customer satisfaction?

When it comes to making customers happy, we should always try our best. Yet we must also be sensitive to the needs of our construction department. While we are sometimes shooting at the moving targets of happiness and satisfaction, they are shooting at a stationary target – building their homes correctly and on time. They cannot afford unlimited disruption. This means we need to find a stationary target we can shoot at, too. What is that target? It is the target of ***meeting or exceeding all of the expectations that we set***. If we set the correct expectations up front, and commit ourselves to meeting or exceeding these expectations, we will go a long way in the direction of customer satisfaction. After all, the expectations we set are the only ones for which we can be fully responsible. We cannot take responsibility for expectations buyers have created in their own minds that run counter to our way of building homes and doing business. We can only do our best to help them adjust those expectations to the reality of what we are providing.

How can we set the right expectations that will result in high levels of customer satisfaction?

Know the correct expectations to set for your customers.

Setting correct expectations begins with everyone in the company reaching agreement on what those expectations should be.

Ask your sales manager for this guidance, and then talk to your superintendent to see if he or she agrees. If there are any discrepancies, do whatever you can to get them resolved. Perhaps a group meeting between the sales and construction departments, and anyone else with valuable input, would be appropriate. It is vital to your success and that of your company that there be a consistent understanding throughout the company of what expectations you should be setting. After all, your shoulders are where the expectations challenge ultimately rests.

Remember that you are selling a process as well as a product.

When customers buy a home from you, they are buying not only a product, but also a process. In addition to the design, features, location, community, home site and builder, customers are also buying the way you do business. Your process would include the following elements:

- Your procedure for selling a home, including getting your customers to accept your sales contract the way it is.
- Your procedure for helping customers secure a loan, especially when your builder has an in-house lender or a preferred lender.
- Your procedure for choosing options, including cutoff dates.
- Your construction process (including your specifications, construction schedule, customer inspections, and your level of flexibility with respect to customizing and closing dates).
- Your system for handling the needs, requests and complaints of your customers during the construction process.

We sometimes do a better job of selling our product than we do of selling our process. But if we cannot do a good job of selling both, we have not really made a sale. The customer may agree to buy one of our homes, but we will need to be prepared for the customer to be disappointed eventually. Disappointing a customer with our process can have consequences that are just as serious as disappointing them with our product. Setting correct expectations of product and process are both critical to achieving customer satisfaction.

At some point no later than the contract visit, you need to have a conversation with the buyer in which you say, *"Let me explain how the process works from this point on."* In this conversation you would set their expectations for the items listed with bullets above.

We live in a society where, in any business, **the seller always dictates the process.** Therefore, this expectation is already there, as long as we don't erode it. Terms may be negotiable, but only the seller determines the process, never the buyer. Sometimes we feel reluctant in this matter. After all, they are spending so much money. But we are the builder, and we have a process we believe in. Our process is what has made us successful. We need to stick with this process in order for it to work. As long as we demonstrate our belief in our process with confidence, we are on safe ground. It is when we show doubts in our own process that the customers' confidence begins to erode. They may want to dictate our process from time to time. That is a natural result of the anxiety that accompanies such a large purchase. But they have made an agreement (or they should have) to buy our home the way we build it. If they are unwilling to make that agreement, then all bets are off.

The better we explain the purpose and benefits of our system – why we do it our way and not someone else's – the better we build confidence in our buyers and set correct expectations, even when we don't give customers what they are demanding.

Create a relationship of mutual responsibility with your customers.

You always want to convey a "win-win" attitude to your customers. This is a relationship which is intended to be good for everyone. Part of this win-win attitude includes an atmosphere of mutual responsibility. This is part of your effort to set correct expectations at the outset. You are explaining to customers what their expectations of you should be, but also what expectations you have of them as the process progresses from the sales contract to the final closing. The relationship needs to be established from the outset as a level playing field. You have explained to your customers what your responsibilities are to them, but also what their responsibilities are to you. If they have concerns or unwillingness regarding any of those responsibilities, it is best to get these issues out on the table as early as possible so they can be addressed.

There is nothing to be intimidated about here. Customers already have this expectation, so all we have to do is fulfill it. The worst that could happen would be that the customer responds, "Listen here. I'm spending a lot of money, so I'll tell you how it works, you won't tell me." But even then, if you have this situation, the sooner you know it, the better. If you don't deal with it decisively in the first place, you will deal with it every day from that point on.

Many people want someone else to take responsibility when things get difficult. Unfortunately, this includes some of our customers. They may make a wrong choice about an optional item, or lock in their loan too soon, or give a premature closing date on their resale. When their plans hit a bump in the road, they want you to take responsibility. They may even lay guilt upon you, which can be a very powerful weapon for customers to wield. This is when it is important go back to the original expectation you set, so you can say, *"I'm afraid we won't be able to make that change at this point, but we will do everything we said we'd do."* Naturally, if you can accommodate their request, then life is perfect. But if you cannot, your conscience must be clear that this is their responsibility and not yours. But make sure they realize it is their responsibility up front. For situations involving changes and scheduling, a gentle proactive conversation at the time of purchase that says, "We will take responsibility for _____, but you will need to take responsibility for _____ " should not cause any problems. Customers expect to have responsibilities when they buy. They just sometimes want to shed them later on.

Be consistent.

It is often said that it is harder to set expectations for upscale buyers because they are more demanding. Actually, there are demanding buyers in all price ranges, just as there are easy-to-please ones. Perhaps it is not so much that upscale buyers are more demanding as it is that they are more persistent. After all, persistence is perhaps what made them successful, and therefore affluent. If they feel it is important for them to be **persistent**, then it is equally important for you to be **consistent**.

A vital part of setting correct expectations and then meeting or exceeding those expectations is being consistent. This is another reason it is so important for you, your managers and your construction people to be reading off the same page. If customers go over your head or around you, be sure they get the same answer from whomever they talk to.

Likewise, stay consistent with your previous answers. Sometimes it is right and necessary to say, "Well, okay, I'll check on it and see if we can make a change." Just realize that in addition to accommodating your customer, you are also rewarding their persistence. *Everything we do with our customers trains them how to treat us the next time.* We need to be sure *we train them before they train us.*

HANDLING CUSTOMER CHALLENGES

One of the greatest joys in new home sales is helping customers improve their lives. You can make a significant difference in the well-being of many people by using your expertise and your temperament to help them through a difficult, complex decision. This is a wonderful source of career fulfillment that most professions cannot provide.

Psychologists say that moving to a new home ranks behind death of loved ones and divorce as the third most stressful situation that people experience in our society, not counting extraordinary personal catastrophes. Helping people through this kind of stress and confusion is one of the gifts we can offer.

There are times when the unique stresses of a new home transaction can create adversity between us and a customer. We are not the customer's enemy, but rather their ship's captain whose courage and expertise can guide them through the stormy waters. We need to maintain our hope that harmony can be restored if everyone's dignity can be maintained during times of adversity. We are still allies pursuing a common goal, just in different ways.

Customers are no more perfect than we are. There are times when they will see our flaws, and times when we will see theirs. Most of us want to be good people. However, many people have difficult behavior patterns. At some point in your career you will occasionally deal with customers who possess one or more of the following characteristics: unreasonable, overly demanding, controlling, manipulative, anxiety-ridden, indecisive or dishonest. Everyone deserves a home, and you always want to provide the best service you can. But you also need to protect yourself and your company.

When you are faced with these kinds of customer challenges, attitude is critical. It is very important that you not allow difficult customers to take a toll on you. Knowing how to cope with difficult customers will help you sustain the joy and fulfillment your career provides, and maintain a healthy perspective over the long term.

Protect the customer's dignity as well as your own when difficult situations arise.

No matter how difficult a customer may be, it is important to preserve their dignity. They are entitled to this by virtue of being a customer. Likewise, you are entitled to your dignity by virtue of being a professional. When a customer attacks your dignity, you can protect it by not reacting to the attack, but by being gentle and maintaining your high standards. Tell yourself they simply don't cope well with the stress of life-changing decisions. Your job is to help them get through it. If you do, they will appreciate you later. In most cases you should not take their attack personally. You can say to yourself, "This is not about me. It is about them."

Maintain a consistent pattern of behavior with difficult customers, as with all others.

If difficult customers see you waffling, they will take advantage of it. If you say you will not negotiate, and then say you will, you will open a can of worms that is very hard to close back up. Customers want to see consistency, perhaps even more than they want to get their own way. One of the most fascinating aspects of selling homes is balancing the fact that customers want what they want with the fact that they also want to see strength and confidence in your position. They want you to meet their demands, and yet they do not want to see you tossed about in the slightest wind of adversity. Consistency shows that you are confident, and that you really believe in what you are doing. It also helps them realize that you really want to be fair to all of your buyers. Customers perceive your consistent behavior as a sign that you are successful, and that you take your standards seriously. Most customers realize they will benefit from this approach in the long run, even if your response to a particular demand is not what they originally wanted to hear. They want to know you are sincere about your sense of purpose. Therefore, you must explain your purpose, and the systems that enable you to succeed in your purpose.

Convey a "win-win" attitude to your customers.

When a customer makes a demand that you cannot fulfill, it is perfectly appropriate to say, *"We need to come up with something that works or both of us. It has to be a win-win situation. I want to be fair to you, but I have to be fair to my company, too."* When it looks as though you are trying to put a customer's agenda ahead of the well-being of the company who employs you, it may give the customer a moment of exhilaration, but a delayed reaction of concern and suspicion will likely follow.

*   *   *

Let's consider a variety of customer challenges and apply several principles we have discussed. We will explore ideas for how to handle customers who are angry, those who worry a lot, and the occasional customer who seeks to control or manipulate the relationship. We will also discuss ways to handle construction delays and buyer's remorse. Because these are difficult (and sometimes delicate) subjects, there is a tendency to avoid them or pretend they don't exist. They are certainly the exception, and not the rule. However, we need to be prepared for these situations when they do occur, or we will wind up accidentally mistreating our customers or our builders.

Anxiety is a natural human emotion. During times of anxiety our customers and builders both deserve our understanding and service. To serve both of these parties, we need to maintain control of the situation. This includes maintaining a position of strength with our customers, and training them how to treat us the next time. Either we will set the tone of the relationship or the customer will. The more effectively we can set the tone, the smoother the relationship will be. With each of the topics that follow, we will look at ways to maintain our position of leadership with customers, even during times of adversity.

Angry Customers

Hopefully you will not have to deal with angry customers too often. Yet sooner or later it becomes part of the job for everyone who sells new homes, no matter how good you or your builder may be. Sometimes events seem to conspire to make customer anger a constant and overwhelming challenge. These can be exhausting, depressing times. Sometimes they can even be discouraging enough to cause a salesperson to consider changing careers.

In some situations a customer's anger seems out of line, and others well justified. Let's take the position that it does not matter if the customer's anger is justified or not. We will not be talking about how to solve the problem that caused the anger, but about how to get customers beyond their anger.

When we are confronted by angry customers, we wish we could say something that makes their anger go away immediately so we won't have to deal with it any more. However, anger frequently does not work that way. It often takes longer to subside. In many situations, our realistic goal is not to make them happy on the spot, but to help them find peace after awhile, and give them a way or a reason to accept their situation once they have had a chance to cool off.

Of course, the best way to reduce the possibility of an angry customer is to set the correct expectations up front, and then maintain consistency in your procedures, and in the answers and explanations you give to your customers. But what happens when that does not work? Suppose you have not been able to meet the expectations you set, or the customer gets angry for some other reason. How do you handle the anger in a way that helps the customer get over it?

As we said earlier, the first goal is to protect the dignity of your customer and yourself throughout the confrontation. When we are attacked, we can become consumed with the desire to retaliate. And yet we know this will usually fuel their anger.

We may accidentally fuel their anger by trying to distance ourselves from our company during times of adversity. The word "we" rolls off the tongue easily when we are giving good news. But when the news is bad, we sometimes begin referring to the builder as "they." We come across sounding to the customer as though we no longer support our builder, which validates the customer's anger even further. There are certain situations in which it is right to express empathy with a customer's anger, but acting ashamed is much different from empathy. If we sound ashamed, it can not only fuel our customers' anger, but also their desire to be compensated. Keep your cool as you convey warmth to your customer.

You can show humility, and still show confidence at the same time. You are providing the best service you can, but your service includes being the guide through the jungle of a new home purchase. When a customer attacks you with anger, you don't have to win or lose. You just have to help. Show confidence by explaining to them that it will work out – and how it will. Don't grovel. Stand your ground and maintain your position of strength in the relationship even when you are apologizing. Let them see that you are assuming everything will turn out fine.

I enjoyed watching one particular salesperson's approach to handling angry customers. While she would adapt her approach to each customer and situation, the principles guiding her approach remained consistent. When customers stormed into her sales office with complaints about their homes during construction, her approach would sound something like this:

"I know it's difficult to walk through a home that's being built for you and see mistakes. If I didn't understand how the whole system works, I'd be frustrated, too. What I need for you to understand is that we're prepared for these kinds of mistakes. It's part of the subcontracting process, and you see the same problems in every price range. Builders try to prevent mistakes, but realistically it's just as important to have a good system for correcting them when they do happen. And don't forget, I'm here to help you through this. I'm not going to promise you that everything will be perfect every step of the way, or that mistakes will be corrected immediately. Usually it makes more sense to correct mistakes later, so each subcontractor is in the home as few times as possible. What I can tell you is that we're all watching your home closely, and it will be everything I promised you. As long as we do everything we promised each other, this will have a happy ending, and that's what really matters."

Let's look at some of the highlights of her approach.

- *Empathy* – "I know it's difficult…" Her demeanor conveyed respect and warmth (she always smiled as she responded, no matter how upset the customer was), and maintained everyone's dignity. Yet she never lost the upper hand in her overall tone, and she never groveled.

- *Confidence* – She gently reminded her customers that she and her company were the experts, and the customer was not. ("If I didn't understand how the whole system works, I'd be frustrated, too.") Here she managed to combine her empathy with her position of leadership and expertise. The rest of her explanation built upon this confidence.

- *A Patient Explanation* – She was not abrupt or arrogant in her confidence. She showed that she cared about their concerns, and about them as individuals. She also explained that there was a process, and that she was comfortable in the effectiveness of the process. While being patient and complete, her explanation was not so long-winded as to arouse suspicion.

- *Personal Reassurance* – "I'm here to help you through this." She continued to refer to her company as "we," just as she had done during the selling process.

- *Mutual Responsibility* – "As long as we all do everything we promised each other …" She maintained a position of balance in the relationship when she was threatened with the possibility of being reduced to a position of weakness. She maintained the "adulthood" of the relationship.

- *Perspective* – She helped her customers focus on the bigger picture, the total process, and the fact that a "happy ending" was really what they had purchased.

When dealing with customer anger, you always want to maintain the proactive role. You should provide the solution, not ask the customer what they think the solution should be. Sometimes, in a combination of desperation and good intentions, we say to a customer, "What can we do to make you happy?" Then, suddenly, everything is negotiable, which is only one step away from out of control. If you are blindsided by a customer's anger, or cannot provide a solution on the spot, explain that you need some time to pursue a solution, or simply to get more information in order to give them the best and fairest answer possible. You still do not have to forfeit your position of strength and leadership in the relationship. If you really do owe the customer something for a mistake that has been made, you want to be in the proactive position of saying, "Here is what we would like to do to make this right..."

One of the most difficult situations in dealing with customer anger is when you have made a major mistake that cannot be corrected. In this situation your company may decide to offer some other form of compensation. But sometimes a builder feels that this is not an appropriate solution, or there is no form of compensation that is mutually acceptable. The builder may believe that the only viable option is to offer the customer a refund, and resell the home to someone else. In these situations it is best not to try to snow the customer. Fancy footwork rarely resolves this kind of situation permanently. Only an honest, straightforward, sincere approach can hope to maintain the dignity to which everyone involved in the transaction is still entitled. *"It is our fault, but I'm afraid we can't correct it at this point. I know this is an important issue to you, and a home is an important decision. You owe it to yourself to have a home you'll be happy with. If this is no longer that home, then we will not ask you to continue."*

The Controller

In any new home sales relationship, either you or the customer will set the tone. Whoever sets the tone controls the relationship. In order to gain effective control of the relationship, you need to train the customer before the customer trains you. New home sales transactions run more smoothly when the seller controls the relationship, because the seller is the one who understands the process. Terms may be negotiable. Customers have free will to choose whether or not they will buy. But the buyer never determines the process in any business. That right always belongs to the seller. It is the only way a business can run effectively. It is the only way a seller can set the correct expectations, and then fulfill those expectations.

Most customers do not really want control of the new home sales relationship. They just want us to explain how things will work, and then to do what we say we will do. But some customers are more controlling by nature. They want to control everything in which they are involved. How do we handle the customer who demands control of the relationship? What do we do when a customer says, "I'm paying a lot of money, and when I pay a lot of money, I get what I want."

First we need to recognize when a customer is truly battling for control, as opposed to simply making a request (or even a demand). An isolated request or demand is different from a pattern of controlling behavior. It is when we see a pattern that we realize the customer is truly battling for control. They want us to change our way of doing business in order to accommodate them. They are continually seeking to bend us to their will. When we see the pattern continue to repeat itself, our goal must be to neutralize that pattern as quickly as possible. In our efforts to please the controlling customer, we sometimes inadvertently nurture the controlling behavior pattern. This increases the customer's position of strength and diminishes our own. In doing so, we ironically lower our chances of completing the sale, and then maintaining a satisfied customer.

Our position of strength is an essential part of our success. The best way to maintain the respect of the controlling customer, and the integrity of our operation in their eyes, is to do what we say we will do, remain consistent, and not give them the impression we are willing to sell our soul to make a sale. All of this can be accomplished with our dignity and the dignity of our customers remaining intact. Here are a few ideas of how this can be done.

Don't be afraid to lose the sale.

Customers do not want to see fear in a salesperson. Even controllers want to buy from salespeople who are confident. Although they may not initially believe in the way we do things, they need to see that we do believe in it. Just like any other customer, controllers deserve our patience, our respect, and our best service. They just do not deserve control. Not because they are controllers, but because the only way we can uphold our standards and meet our commitments is by executing the decisions we have already made, and not blowing in a different direction with every gust of wind. And controllers do provide their share of gusts. The more control we give to a controller, the more control they want. It is an insatiable thirst. While we cannot satisfy the thirst, we can provide the antidote – consistency. We can provide credible, knowledgeable answers, and a clear explanation of our mission and purpose.

When you cannot meet all of a controller's needs, it may be that he or she is simply not your customer. You do your best with each opportunity you have, yet your greatest position of strength is sometimes your willingness to lose a sale. Showing that you are not afraid to lose a sale can be the best way to make a sale to a controller. It can also help set a better tone for the relationship that follows the contract.

There may even be times when you need to say to the controller, *"You owe it to yourself to find the home and builder that is best for you. I hope that will be us, but we really believe in the way we do things, and you need to decide if that will work for you."*

Maintain a level playing field.

Your relationships with your customers are like any other adult relationship. They need to be balanced and mutually respectful. If control of the relationship is essential to them, you may have to explain that such an arrangement will not work for you. You can say, *"Our goal is to have a win-win arrangement with all of our customers. It has to work for both of us."* Any successful business relationship requires a balance of mutual expectations and responsibilities. Even controllers understand that principle.

Train your customers how to treat you.

When selling to the controller, it is important to neutralize the behavior pattern and not nurture it. In the buyer-seller relationship, you are continually training your customers how to treat you. Let's take a customer who wants you to jump through hoops by getting them a series of answers to unusual questions or special requests. If they are willing to make a commitment based upon your fulfillment of those requests, that is one thing. However, if they only want you to pursue a series of demands without any offer of commitment in return, you are frequently traveling a tedious road to nowhere, with no one but annoyed co-workers to greet you at the final destination.

If you show customers you are willing to jump through hoops for them without requiring any commitment in return, you are telling them you are willing to indulge their fantasies without achieving any resolution. Unfortunately, there are some customers who enjoy the power of getting people to jump through hoops. They may be control freaks, or they may be pretenders. One of the symptoms of "pretender syndrome" is when a customer says to you, in one way or another, "If you will do for me what I already know you cannot do, I will buy your home." You need to turn that around by finding a way to say to them, "I will pursue your request if you will buy my home." For example, you could say, *"If we can resolve this issue for you, will that make this a home you'll be happy with?...Then let's go ahead and write it up."*

If you cannot accommodate their request, then it is best to deal with that problem head-on, explaining why you cannot do it, and finding out where that leaves them. There is no use dragging out a situation like that.

A similar challenge is the customer who continually wants to renegotiate a contract or make additional demands after it is ratified. Do not fall victim to the idea that customers have the position of strength between contract and closing, and do not train them to think that way either. They were already willing to buy the home without the demands in the first place. Just because they have more time to think after the contract, this does not mean that every new thought should find its way on to the addendum to the purchase agreement. There is nothing wrong with telling a customer that they made an agreement, and gave their word, just as you did. You expect them to honor their word, just as you will. You will not go back to them to renegotiate, and they should not come back to you either.

When a customer stands you up for an appointment to write a contract, think carefully about how much you want to keep chasing them. It is one thing if they call you and have to reschedule. It is quite a different situation when they make an appointment, don't show up, and don't call. How to handle this is a case-by-case decision. There will be times when you want to give it another try. There are other times when you might prefer to leave a message on their answering machine that says, *"I missed you for our appointment today at 10:00. If you would still like to buy the home, please give me a call by 6:00 today so we can reschedule."* Then if you don't hear from them, just move on. If there is any chance of saving the sale, it needs to be with your dignity and position of strength intact in order for the relationship to succeed.

As we said earlier, you need to be the one who sets the tone of the relationship. The more often you reward a customer's negative behavior, the more often you will see it. With the controller, as with any other customer, the best approach is to stick with your program, explaining to your customers why you do it the way you do it, and why you believe in it.

Maintaining control of the relationship is not really so hard. You do not have to win control. As the seller, you already have it. All you have to do is not give it up.

The Manipulator

Manipulation can be harder to deal with than outright anger, because it is gentler and subtler. Sometimes it even feels good to be manipulated, as with flattery. Other times it feels bad, as with guilt. In any case, manipulation needs to be dealt with like other customer challenges – with confidence and consistency.

We mentioned that guilt can be one form of manipulation. In fact, guilt may be a manipulator's most powerful weapon. We can feel devastated when a customer says, "We're just not happy," or, "We trusted you, and you let us down." We want to make it right, and we want to ask the customer how we can do that. Yet this can be a very dangerous road to travel, especially if we are being manipulated.

When guilt is used as a tool of manipulation, it can frequently lead to a request for compensation. Once we show that we feel guilty, suddenly everything becomes negotiable. The customer may take an approach that sounds something like, "We're very disappointed. This whole experience has kept us awake at night. If you can give us _____, we'll feel much better about everything. We may even send you some referrals."

Claims of misunderstanding can be another form of manipulation, and can be used in conjunction with guilt. "When we bought our home, we thought we were getting _____. Now that we're not, we're very disappointed. How are you going to fix this?"

These kinds of situations are among the most difficult we face in new home sales. They frequently present dilemmas for which no solution truly feels right. When these kinds of situations occur one time with a customer, they are disturbing. However, when they repeat themselves with the same customer, we realize we are facing a dangerous behavior pattern, and we must be prepared to handle it.

When you see a behavior pattern that seems manipulative, does that mean the customer is doing it intentionally? In one sense, it doesn't really matter. Whether the behavior pattern is deliberate or accidental, conscious or subconscious, we still have to neutralize it. As with the controller, we have to be able to show a customer that manipulation will not work with us. We will honor our commitments and provide excellent service, but we must still keep the playing field level. We must treat the buyer-seller relationship as an adult one – a relationship in which everyone fulfills the responsibilities to which they have committed.

For many people manipulative behavior seems unconscious, because it comes so naturally. They do not necessarily mean any harm. They just want what they want, and are not too particular about how they get it. For example, they may claim that you made a commitment you did not make. While you want to show your customers you understand and are sensitive to their needs, you do not want to be in doubt as to what has been agreed upon. Part of the job of a new home salesperson is remembering what has been said. Some salespeople have absolute confidence in their ability to remember conversations. Others keep notes as they go in order to have a reference point in case of a misunderstanding. This does not mean you have to write down every word you say. However, you want to keep whatever notes are necessary in order for you to be certain about commitments you have made and information you have conveyed.

There will be times when you will think to yourself, "There is no way I could have said that." If you are certain of the truth, then you need to stick by it. You can say to the customer, *"That's not the kind of commitment I could have made, because I know better,"* or, *"I'm afraid that's not something I could have told you, because I know the truth is different."* These kinds of situations can become especially difficult, because you feel as though you are calling the customer a liar. You must not think of it that way. You are only telling what you know to be true.

You may occasionally find yourself in situations where it seems that the only choices you have are to call a customer a liar or call yourself a liar. However, if the customer has put you in that position, and you know that what they are saying is not true, you have to address it or risk damaging your own credibility. Everything we do with a customer trains them how to treat us the next time. If we show customers that we will cave on every misunderstanding, we will have trained them which button to push when they feel they need to. Unfortunately, it is just not true that "the customer is always right." However, when they are, we need to take our medicine and fix the problem by adhering to the standard of "doing the right thing."

How do you know when you are being manipulated? If you feel yourself losing control because customers seem to be wrapping you around their fingers to the point that you are giving them things you know they are not entitled to, then it needs to be addressed as manipulation. Whether the manipulation is intentional or not, your goal is to get the relationship back to a level playing field. As with all other customer challenges, you want to be caring and empathetic. However, you also need to reinforce the concept of *mutual responsibility*. If you are doing everything you said you would do, and are meeting every expectation you set, then you have earned the right to expect the same from your customers.

Of course, there will be times when a customer really is entitled to something, even if it was not previously agreed upon. For whatever reason, you have come up short on your commitments, and you feel that some sort of compensation is necessary in order to make things right. If compensation may be involved (as in the case of a mistake that cannot be corrected or a customer who is temporarily out on the street through the fault of your builder), then the remedy becomes a corporate decision. However, in situations where compensation is not appropriate, it is usually better to say this to the customer right up front. For example, *"I know this is an inconvenience, but we can't compensate every time an inconvenience occurs. We want you to be happy in your home, but these things do happen, and it's really not a compensation issue."* We do not want to train our customers that inconvenience equals compensation.

Still, there are times when a company decides that compensation is simply the right thing to do.

A manipulator may decide to tell other people in your company that you promised them something when you didn't. Everyone who may become involved with a customer needs to be on the same page regarding the expectations you set and the commitments you make. If a customer tells a construction person or a manager that you have promised them something, that person can respond to the customer by saying, *"Let me check with _____ (the salesperson) on this, and either she or I will get back to you."*

If you take over a community from a salesperson who has left the company, you may face claims from customers concerning promises made by the salesperson who has left. Suppose you find no record of such a commitment in your file, and now it is too late to make a change. This is another situation in which the straight and narrow path is usually the best one. Unless your company tells you they will honor these verbal commitments, you will likely find yourself in the uncomfortable position of telling the customer "no." One way to do this is by saying, *"Everything we agree to that involves building your home has to be done in writing, because that's the only way we can process the item. I'm afraid I don't have anything in the file, so there's really no way I can pursue it at this point."* Customers actually do understand this. Naturally, if they have a copy of an agreement in writing, then it needs to be honored.

Sometimes we have customers who seem perpetually confused. For some people, confusion can be another form of manipulation. Again, there is a difference between a person who gets confused once and a person who gets confused about everything. If you have a customer who continually claims to be confused, and then follows their expression of confusion with a request for something special, this is a pattern, and therefore a danger signal. It is similar to the pattern of "misunderstandings" we discussed earlier, except that the confused person tends to jump around more from one issue to the next, and is not necessarily trying to arouse guilt. They are just confused, and yet you wonder how they could be.

Sometimes "confusion" results from a reluctance to make commitments or honor them. They key is to not allow yourself to be caught up in the customer's confusion. Trust in your own ability to communicate information clearly and accurately. Then you can respectfully say, *"I'm sorry this has been confusing for you. The way it works is _____. This is the way we do it for everyone."* Then stick to your game plan.

The Worrier

We are always thankful for those customers who are willing to trust us. However, there are others who appear consumed with anxiety, and there seems to be no way we can get them to trust us. Their worry seems part pessimism and part suspicion. We want to be respectful of them, of their needs, and even of their worries. If we show disrespect for their worries, it will probably only make them worry more. But if we sympathize too much, that could make them worry more, too. How do we show just enough empathy to maintain the stability of the relationship without nurturing the troublesome behavior pattern? We want to take their concerns seriously, but we also want to help them find a safe place in their minds to keep their worries. We need to help them discover the correct perspective for their worries.

One way to do this is through proactive communication. If they are serious worriers, you will probably know it by the time they sign their contract. The first step in reducing worry is to be especially careful to set correct expectations at the contract. Tell them you will keep in touch with them – that you will keep them updated on the status of their home, and that you will check in with them on a consistent basis. Also let them know that things can go wrong, and that you have a process for fixing them when they do. You don't have to go overboard by telling them, "If you have any concerns, call me day or night." Just go through a normal procedure of explaining how things work, just as you would with any other customer. Don't treat them as special cases. The more you do, the more you will nurture the behavior pattern you are trying to neutralize. You can be patient and understanding without becoming so sympathetic that you make them feel their worries are justified.

In some cases you may even decide to directly address the idea that their worry is related to trust, and that they will need to trust you in order for the relationship to continue smoothly. Explain to them that buying a home, and then watching it be built, can be anxiety-producing, and that you are there to handle their worries so they don't have to. Say to them, *"I'm going to ask you to trust me on this."* There are times when putting it on a personal level in this way is the most effective approach you can take.

You may need to walk through their home a little more often during the construction process to make sure everything is okay. Then, if there is something wrong, you can show them you are proactive, that you are on top of the situation, and that you already have a solution.

Sometimes anecdotes of other buyers can help an overly worried customer become more confident. Tell about other people who got themselves tied up in knots with worry, and then everything worked out okay after all. Once they moved in, they admitted to you they had wasted a lot of time and energy with their worries. You could tell about others who never worried because they knew that was your job. They enjoyed the whole process much more. Either way, problems do happen, and they do get solved. Buyers move in and are happy with their homes. The point of your anecdotes is to say, "You will be happy when this is over." You can counsel them with this advice: *"You shouldn't be putting yourself through so much turmoil. You need to enjoy this time. Buying a new home should be a source of happiness, not worry."*

In extreme cases you may make the decision to offer the customer a refund rather than continue with a problem that seems impossible to solve. When the customer's worry becomes so overwhelming, so constant and so destructive that you feel you need to present this option to the customer, you can say, *"Don't put yourself through this. If this is a decision that is going to make you miser-*

able, then it's going to make me miserable, too." You can continue to reinforce the positives of buying your home. But you are also saying, *"If you feel that buying this home is a mistake, then we need to fix it, and we are willing to work with you in order to do that. If you think it's not a mistake, then you need to trust us to do the job you're paying us to do. We will do everything we said we would do, just as we have for everyone else here."*

Construction Delays

Construction delays can be one of the most stressful parts of a new home salesperson's job. Customers get more and more frustrated, and we feel more and more helpless. We feel our credibility slipping away, and sometimes our joy along with it. Here we will look at two issues related to handling customer anxiety in the face of construction delays:

1. How can we prepare customers for delays in advance?

2. How can we handle customers once delays occur?

Ironically, one of our greatest assets is the building industry's notorious reputation for delays. The expectation is already out there. All we have to do is figure out how to use this expectation to our advantage.

Everyone involved in the transaction has their own responsibility. While you have responsibility for trying to meet your schedule, customers have responsibility for planning their lives according to the *real* information available. Once you have explained the schedule, stage by stage, and the risks involved, their decisions that concern giving notice to their landlord, promising a settlement date to their resale buyer, and locking in their interest rate must be their responsibility, not yours. They know that you do not have complete control over the construction schedule of a home, especially one that is not yet under roof. They are getting the benefits of a new home (newer design and technology, a warranty, personalized selections, and a home that has never been occupied by someone else), but there may be potential inconveniences. The inconveniences pass, but the benefits last for years. Customers already understand this. Yet sometimes they want us to take responsibility when they make an error in judgment involving some other commitment. The better we are at explaining the building process and setting the right expectations at the beginning, the more we can reduce our responsibility for things that are not really our fault.

Our goal is always to set realistic expectations without putting sales at risk. But when a customer demands a promise from us that we should not make, we are better off addressing the issue once up front than every day for the next several months. *"I would love to be able to promise the future, but any salesperson who does that is selfishly putting customers at risk. It's better to address the possibility of an inconvenience now, and be prepared for it. Even if an inconvenience does occur, and we hope it doesn't, it will only be temporary, while the home is permanent. I can tell you we have a very good process, and we try to be realistic in order to be sensitive to our customers. But in any business when something has not yet been delivered, there is always some risk of the unforeseen. We're good at dealing with the unforeseen, but we can't always prevent it. I want to be as honest as I can about that right up front, so you can prepare your end of things accordingly."*

Customers should appreciate this kind of approach. They want care and honesty, not just fast talk. However, when a customer demands something that you are probably unable to deliver, it is just like any other "offer." If they are not willing to work within your system and terms, it simply may not be a sale. It is better to address it honestly at the beginning than be held hostage by it later.

At what point do you tell customers their home is behind schedule? In general, you want to have this conversation as early and as few times as possible. Naturally, the conversation is easier if you have set the right expectations up front. But if you have not, try to maintain the right perspective in order to help your buyers do the same. If there is possible cost or inconvenience to the buyer, the issue should not be handled flippantly. On the other hand, construction delays are not life-threatening, even when customers have to move into temporary housing or put their furniture in storage. As we said, the earlier you can let them know the better. But if the delay takes you by surprise, talk to your company first to see if they are willing to offer any form of compensation. If they are not, then go into the conversation with as much dignity as possible, giving a complete, honest explanation and the appropriate apology. Then realize that the customer's anger is a temporary moment in a world of much larger and longer-term problems.

Buyer's Remorse

We know that buyer's remorse can be a normal part of the buying process, but many customers don't know it. Natural feelings of second-guessing snowball into panic. Suddenly the buyer wants out.

No matter how well you sell, how much trust and rapport you create, and how thoroughly you help your buyers through a complete decision process, a certain amount of buyer's remorse will be inevitable. Some of it will even be incurable.

There are several reasons why you will never be able to completely eliminate buyer's remorse. One reason is that there will always be some people who simply cannot handle large decisions. Their tendency to bail out on commitments is a life-long pattern of behavior. There will also be occasional situations where the buyer's decision to purchase really was a mistake, for reasons that you might never fully understand. You did nothing wrong. You did not coerce them into something that is not in their best interests. They decided that buying a home was the right thing to do. Then they changed their minds and decided it was not.

If you rarely see buyer's remorse in your customers, don't change your selling approach just because it happens occasionally. However, if you feel you need to change something in your approach in order to lower your buyer's remorse cancellations, here are a few ideas to consider.

Some salespeople like to have a conversation on the day of the contract in which they directly address the issue of buyer's remorse. If you feel a proactive conversation might help, here is an example of how to approach it:

"Congratulations. This is a wonderful community, and people are very happy here. I know what a relief it is to get a decision like this completed, and you've picked a terrific home. As with any big decision, there's usually a moment later on when you say, 'Am I really sure about this?' With buying a home, that feeling seems to last a day or two, and then when it's over a tremendous feeling of contentment sets in. But if you have any questions, I'm here for you. I want to thank you again for buying a home from me. I know you'll love it, and I look forward to having you as a neighbor."

Whether you choose to have a preventive conversation or not, it is important to give the customer a follow up call a day or two after the contract. Some salespeople prefer the combination of a note and a call. It is a chance to thank them once more and show them that you value them as customers. It is important that the whole experience "feel right" to the customer – before, during and after the contract.

If buyer's remorse does occur, there will be times when there is nothing you can do. However, your best bet is still to remain calm and gracious. If you are trying to restore the customer's comfort level, the first thing they need to see is your own comfort level. As the saying goes, "never let them see you sweat."

Whether their request to cancel is over the phone or in person, maintain your respect for them, and move the conversation in the direction of reliving the day they bought the home. *"The day you bought your home, you were so happy. It was a joy to see. I remember you saying* _____ [Recall some specific expression of their joy or certainty with the home]. *Everything seemed so right. It is a huge decision, and second thoughts are a part of any decision that large. Why don't you take another day or two to make sure? After all the time and effort you put into making the right decision in the first place, at least be sure you put as much thought into this one."*

You also want to try to find out if there are any issues that have not been addressed. It is okay to ask that question forthrightly at this point. Sometimes a gesture of patience and graciousness during a moment when they may be feeling a little ashamed of themselves, combined with another day or two to regain their balance, may be enough to get them over this hurdle. However, don't let it stretch out. It will not do them or you any good to look as if you're trying to "salvage the deal."

If your attempts to help them overcome their buyer's remorse fail, it is best to just say to yourself, "It happens. It's not a 'lost sale.' It's just a home that will wind up with a different owner."

Conquering Slumps

All salespeople are vulnerable to slumps – even those with a mentality for success. While a mentality for success may not be enough to enable you to avoid slumps altogether, it can help you end your slumps more quickly. Here are several ideas to incorporate into your success mentality, so that you can attack your slumps in a positive way when they do occur.

GET BACK INTO THE ZONE

When you are at your best, everything you do seems to work perfectly. Selling homes seems simple and easy. Every interaction seems joyful. Every word you say has positive impact. You feel as though you are *in the zone.*

Being in the zone is the opposite of being in a slump. When you are in a slump, everything seems difficult and complicated. Every interaction feels like a struggle. You feel helpless, as though you are not able to have any impact at all.

The problem with being in the zone is that it seems like an unconscious state. You may have no idea how you got into the zone in the first place, or how to get back into it if you slip out. If only there were a conscious way to get yourself out of a slump and back into the zone.

Perhaps there is!

When you are in the zone, you feel confident in your ability to have a significant positive impact on every customer you meet. You know you are able to motivate them, empower them and lead them. You realize you are a person who can influence others by providing a powerful, enriching experience that is uniquely your own. No one else can provide the special experience you provide when you are at your best.

When you are in a slump, and are not providing that rich, uplifting experience, you still have the ability to envision it – to recreate it in your mind. Imagine yourself through the customer's eyes. What is it they experience when you are at your best? Why do people like to buy homes from you? What is it about yourself that makes you feel you are the best salesperson in the world during those times when you are in the zone? You can retrieve this unique gift consciously, even when you are in a slump.

When you are in the zone, you not only realize why people choose you to be their salesperson, you also have a clear, uncluttered idea of why they choose your homes over everyone else's. You know exactly why your homes are the best ones for the money. When you are in a slump, however, your market position feels much more vulnerable. With so many ways to lose a sale, and so many competitors who can snatch them away, every opportunity seems like a long shot.

Just as you are able to retrieve your vision of why customers want to buy homes from you, you can also retrieve your understanding of why people choose your homes over those of your competition. Recalling the reasons people choose your homes can help you regain confidence in the strength of your market position. Once you have restored your confidence and clarity about what makes your homes the obvious first choice, make sure you convey it to every customer as part of your selling message. A slump is when you need your selling message the most; yet it is also when your selling message is most likely to slip away. Naturally you don't want your selling message to sound canned and repetitious. But remember, it is not repetitious to your customers. They are hearing it for the first time.

Another characteristic of being in the zone is that your relationships with customers seem to keep moving forward more easily. This is no fluke. When you are in the zone, your momentum goes from one stage of the sale to the next more naturally. When you come to a potential stalling point, you keep it going by saying something as simple as, *"The next thing I need to tell you about (show you) (ask you) is..."* You don't ask yourself whether or not to keep going. You just take the attitude that "If the customer is still here, that means they want to keep going."

When you are in a slump, say to yourself, "Keeping the sale moving is the easiest thing in the world. If the customer wants to stop, they'll tell me. Otherwise, we'll just keep going. No matter what happens, I will never be the one who stops the sale."

We have discussed three ways to consciously retrieve the unconscious state of joy, simplicity and clarity known as "the zone."

1. Recall and envision the unique experience you offer your customers that engages them, encourages them, and makes them feel confident and comfortable buying a home from you.

2. Recall and articulate why people choose your homes. Stay focused on why you win sales instead of why you lose them.

3. Don't stop the sale.

RECORD YOUR SUCCESSES

Some salespeople keep a journal of their successes. Every time they make a sale, they write down why they believe they won that sale away from everyone else. This analysis would not only include the competitive advantages of the package you are offering, but also what you believe you did that made a difference – how you helped them appreciate your home enough to buy it, how you helped them progress through the decision process, and how you closed the sale.

Reviewing this journal can be rejuvenating, especially during a slump. It reminds you how great you really are. It enables you to refocus on ways that your knowledge, skills, resourcefulness, and the experience you provide for your customers have given you the competitive edge in the past. You are still the same person who achieved those victories, and you can do it again – perhaps even better.

AT WHAT STAGE IS THE SALES EFFORT STOPPING?

We have discussed that "only the customer should stop the sale, never the salesperson." However, we also know that most of our interactions do stop before becoming a sale. Looking back on the period of the slump, do you see any pattern in where your selling interactions stopped? Is this pattern different from where most of them stop when you are selling well? If there is no difference, then your slump may be just a fluke. You may spring back out of it as quickly as you slipped into it, with no apparent explanation. We see this in baseball when a .300 hitter goes through a period of hitting line drives straight to fielders, or long fly balls that get caught on the warning track. There are times when you do everything right and it just doesn't work. It is important to realize that this situation is possible. In these cases, don't change anything. Don't press. Just relax. Remember that you love to sell, and you're good at it. Don't overthink the slump. Don't try to "force" rapport. Remember that in your better times you were successful not because you were technically perfect, but because you simply loved to sell.

On the other hand, if you do find a particular stage of the sale where your interactions are stopping more frequently than they used to, then focus on getting to, and through, that stage without changing anything else. For example, you may find that you are getting fewer people to home sites than you used to. In this case, you would focus on getting more customers out to the sites, and then making sure you are as effective at that stage of the sale as you used to be. Remember that your goal is always to get to the next stage of the selling process. You also want to be sure you are getting as many customers as possible to those stages of the process you like best, and at which you feel you are most effective.

IF YOU ACT ENTHUSIASTIC, YOU WILL BECOME ENTHUSIASTIC

During a slump it can sometimes take tremendous will to act enthusiastic. But it is important to force yourself. It really is true that we can make ourselves *feel* more excited by *acting* more excited. Also, enthusiasm is contagious. If your customer captures your enthusiasm, you will in turn capture theirs, and the cycle snowballs.

Every customer offers a fresh opportunity to break out of a slump. They don't know you're in a slump. Think of each customer as the one who may end your slump, and just take them as far as you can in the selling process. Make a game of it if it helps. Think of a reward to give yourself for every customer you get to a certain point. If you have another salesperson working alongside you, they can become part of the game as well.

IDEAS TO REVIEW

Several of the ideas we discussed in previous chapters can be helpful for bringing slumps to an end.

DON'T GIVE UP TOO EASILY

If your homes do not appear at first to be exactly what a customer is looking for, remember that a customer's needs can be a moving target. Their needs and plans can change when they find a home they really want.

This idea can also apply to objections. We can become more discouraged by objections when we are in a slump than if we are on a roll. Find out how important the objection is, explain why you created your home the way you did, and remain hopeful that the customer may accept the objection if your home is still better for them overall than anyone else's home. Customers will often accept what they don't want in order to get what they do want.

UNDERSTAND YOUR HOMES' UNIQUE VALUE, AND BELIEVE IN IT

Don't feel discouraged if a customer wants to negotiate more than you are able to. It doesn't mean you have a value problem. Make sure your customers understand the unique way your company defines value at your community. Focus on subjective value as well as objective value.

A success mentality includes an abundance mentality. There are always reasons why customers may not buy your homes, and you will always "lose" sales. But you will still win your share. While it is important to analyze your competitive position to see if any adjustments are necessary, be careful if you are doing this when you are in a slump. You do not have to beat your competition on every feature plus price in order to win a sale. We remember this principle easily enough when we are on a roll, but sometimes it slips away from us when we are in a slump.

DON'T TRY TO FORCE RAPPORT

When rapport does not develop easily, use time as your friend and let it evolve. Try to keep the relationship as light and easy as possible. Rapport can be built as easily through trust as through charisma. Also remember that while some customers may not be willing to talk right away, they may be willing to listen.

STAY FOCUSED ON DECISIONS

Create a decision-making rhythm throughout your relationships with your customers, so that when the time comes to ask for the sale, it will be as easy, obvious and natural as possible. Ask questions along the way to learn their needs and get their feedback.

Sometimes during a slump we feel less confident about closing. Remember that a customer's response is not about their acceptance or rejection of you. Throughout the selling process you are helping your customers resolve a decision they are trying to resolve. Closing is simply inviting your guest to become a homeowner. Your customers should feel as though you want them more than your competitors do. This idea applies to follow up as it does to closing.

YOU ALWAYS HAVE THE POSITION OF STENGTH

A slump can leave you feeling as though you have lost your position of strength. During these times you may need a positive thought in order to recapture your feeling of strength in your relationships with your customers. Consider this: *You can always sell your home to another customer, but they can only buy your home from you.* Naturally, this principle only applies if they want your home, so that must remain your top priority.

A FEW MORE POINTS

- Salespeople with a positive attitude and a sense of humor generally turn a slump around faster than others. There is truth to the cliché, "You're only in a slump as long as you think you're in a slump."

- Use your spare time to help you break out of your slump. Study new sales techniques, especially books and tapes. Attend a seminar or two, if possible. Prepare new strategies and anecdotes you can incorporate to liven up your presentation.

- Are you tired, mentally or physically? If so, you may need to make rest (or a full vacation) your top priority in order for your slump to end.

- Envision the end of your slump. Project your mind into the future, and form an image of what it will be like when your slump ends. Picture yourself selling to a customer after your slump is over (or before it began). Sometimes you wonder if you will ever emerge, but you know you will. Imagine yourself looking back saying, "Why was I so worried?" Your second wind will always kick in, just as it has in the past.

- Finally, remember that you are in a good business performing a valuable service that improves and enriches the lives of many people.